I0558633

STAR KEY

By: Kristina Whitmeyer

TABLE OF CONTENTS

For George
I Love you.

PROJECT KEY SUMMARY

Due to overpopulation and pollution, President ███ has issued Project Key. Project key will be executed by the company ██████. Citizens will be assigned a floor according to their finances and social standing. The board selected four sectors for citizen relocation. Ocean Sector (-3,632 m) location Atlantic and Pacific Oceans. Land (0m) Sector location on Continents. Cloud Sector (45,456m) location Stratosphere. Star Sector (4535,729m) location Exosphere. President ███ decided to relocate the wealthiest ███ to the Star Sector. Star Sector applicants must have a minimum income of █████ to qualify for relocation. Business class and merchants will be stationed in to the Cloud sector. Farmers and the middle class will be moved to the Land Sector. Anyone with an income below $15,000 or marked undesirable will be sent to the Ocean Sector. The project's estimated end date is June 16, ████

Chapter 1

BALLROOM

Luna pressed the cracked five button on the keypad. The decrepit machinery whirled in protest as she was transported upward. She adjusted her faded violet dress and pushed back her black curls. Flies lazily crawled on the dull, yellow bulb above as the elevator came to a stop. Loud, rhythmic beats and electric blue flashes greeted her as the doors creaked open. Luna dug her purple nails into the metallic purse in apprehension and entered the ballroom.

Luna weaved her way around a sea of dancing people. They swayed in unison to the electronic drone of the bass. She marveled at the tiny fairy lights that twinkled softly on the ceiling and the large school of tuna swam past the portholes at the ballroom's perimeter. The people on the dancefloor wore ornate outfits inspired by ocean life and displayed dramatic hairstyles covered in plastic gems. Luna started to feel queasy from the moldy smell that lingered in the air and the sensation of her silver boots colliding with the sticky floor. However, the excitement that buzzed in her head kept her moving towards the neon bar. She sat down and directed her attention to the stage at the

1

center of the dance floor. The crowd went silent as the music grew louder.

Luna gasped as a six-foot queen with wild, green hair and matching heels fell out of the ceiling. The queen elegantly landed in a split and struck a pose, emphasizing her flashy makeup. Stringy vines and flowers engulfed every inch of her body. She reminded Luna of an earth goddess who lived in the Land Sector fifty floors above. The queen sprang into a flip and started her coordinated dance routine. The crowd erupted into cheers. Many banged their towering totems on the tile floor. Others frantically fanned themselves and whispered jealous comments to their friends. Memories of Darnelle and the ballroom flooded back into her mind. She stared at the rainbow lights near the bottles, watching them grow blurry as she fought back tears. A large hand with yellow and black nails gently landed on her own. Luna jolted out of her memories and looked up at Beatrice.

"The usual," the husky bartender asked.

"No, I think I'll have a lemon twist," Luna responded.

"Ahhh, Darnelle's favorite," Beatrice stated as she typed into the register. Luna smiled weakly and secretly hoped Beatrice wouldn't ask her what was wrong. She felt hollow and lost after her brother's death. She knew Darnelle wouldn't want her moping around forever, but losing him was hard.

Beatrice smiled back sympathetically as if she understood. Luna noticed she was sporting new

2

golden earrings and a long, emerald sequin dress that shimmered in the violet light. Luna was about to compliment her, but the woman beside her interrupted.

"Excuse me, I want to place an order, " the woman demanded. Her voice was nasally and proper. Beatrice squeezed Luna's hand, winked, and walked away, promptly ignoring the woman's request. She glided across the bar and started mixing ingredients.

"That's the fifth time she's passed me," the woman protested. Luna looked over. The woman next to her was glamorous and wealthy. She wore a white dress with a matching headband that slicked back her long blond hair. A large diamond ring rested on her finger, and thin gold bracelets clinked around her thin wrist. However, her face was oddly smooth and rubbery looking. Her neck was also wrinkled and reminded Luna of a turkey wattle. She made Luna feel uneasy. Therefore, she decided it would be best to be polite.

"Beatrice can be stubborn sometimes when it comes to new people," Luna explained diplomatically.

"You'll have to forgive her."

"Where I come from, the staff provide exceptional service and most certainly do not ignore their paying customers," the woman huffed.

Luna understood why Beatrice was avoiding this woman. She was not from this floor and probably ranked above anyone in this room. Saying the wrong thing could end badly. Luna softened her face and put on a demure smile.

"Where are you from?" she inquired politely. The woman paused for a second, deep in thought, and then answered.

Floor 152.

"Wow, that must have been a long trip," Luna pointed out, trying to suppress the shock in her voice.

What brings you down here?

The woman's eyes filled with tears, and she erupted into sobs. Luna signaled for Beatrice to get another drink and pulled out a tissue from her purse. The woman nodded in thanks and wiped her eyes.

"I'm sorry, things with my life are just a mess," she apologized. First, our finances, now Jennifer, and my stupid husband. I just can't get anything to go right. I was just hoping to have a change of scenery. Luna handed Beatrice a blue key card for the drinks and put in another order.

"Well, you came to the right place," Luna reassured. All sorts of people come here, but I think you are the first person I've met who lives above floor fifty. Luna handed the woman a lilac drink decorated with a cherry and a festive umbrella.

"Plus, we have these to forget all our worries," Luna continued cheerfully, holding up her drink. They are my brother's favorite.

"Will he be joining us?" the woman asked.

"No, he's no longer here," Luna said, looking at her drink.

Well, I owe you my thanks.

4

"You're the only person who has spoken to me or shown me any kindness," the woman said. I was beginning to think everyone here hates me.

They don't hate you. "They're just afraid," Luna replied.

"Why would they be afraid?" the woman questioned with a puzzled expression.

Luna thought carefully about her response. She felt conflicted about being honest with this woman. "They think that if they offend you, you could have them punished," Luna responded. We don't know people in the Star Sector well and don't want to offend you by accident. So, it's just easier to avoid the situation altogether.

"What, that's crazy," the woman remarked.

"It happened to my brother," Luna explained. He corrected one of the managers from floor forty when we were getting audited at work. The manager placed a sixty-day sentence, and he died in prison.

"I've never heard of such a thing," the woman scoffed.

"I just wanted to explain why people here might be scared to talk to you," Luna continued, her voice edged with exasperation. The woman and Luna sampled their beverages in strained silence.

Orange hair spilled over Luna's shoulder, and cheap cotton candy perfume stung her nose. Luna turned around and beamed at her friend.

5

"You look so pretty, Safari, " Luna squeaked as she embraced her friend. I like the new outfit. Safari batted her fake eyelashes.

"Thank you, girl," she said in a deep voice. Look at how good Marquesha did my nails. Safari flexed her crimson claws and wiggled her fingers in glee.

"They look amazing, though I wouldn't be able to grab anything," Luna confessed. Safari let out a loud, boisterous laugh.

What did you think of Distarina? "She's good, right?" Safari chimed, pointing at the stage.

The one in green? Yeah, she's amazing. "I bet Ginger is jealous," Luna observed. She imagined the arrogant queen throwing a tantrum in the dressing room. Safari flashed her a knowing look. The woman next to her cleared her throat.

"Oh, let me introduce you to this lovely lady from the Star Sector," Luna motioned nervously towards the woman. Safari immediately straightened up and held out her hand.

"Nice to meet you," Safari said while shaking her hand. I'll catch you later, girl. "You ladies, enjoy," Safari said, slipping into the crowd. Luna mournfully watched her friend disappear, leaving a trail of glitter behind her.

"Was that a man?" the woman asked in a hushed tone. Luna flinched at the incredibly impolite and bold statement but quickly recovered.

I have no idea what you're talking about. "All I see is a lovely biological woman," Luna replied, resisting the urge to throttle the woman. Luna hated it when people would speak ill of her best friend. This woman was no exception.

Your skin looks amazing. "How do you keep it looking so healthy," Luna lied. The woman smiled, happy for the change in subject.

"My cousin Jennifer gave me a jar of Junjurikin cream on my 50th birthday. It works miracles, but it was more of a mean-spirited jab on my appearance than an actual gift.

"Wait, doesn't Junjurikin use whale semen as one of their ingredients?" Luna implored, giggling.

"Yes, but you can't ignore its amazing anti-aging properties," the lady defended. I mean, everyone I know uses it. There's no sense in looking old.

"Well, I don't think you need it," Luna argued. I don't see any gray, and you look like you're in your thirties.

"Aww, you are too kind," the woman cooed. You should tell my sister that.

So, your sister and cousin's names are Jennifer. "That must be confusing for your family," Luna pointed out.

"Where I come from, if you have blond hair, you are named Debbie, and if you are a brunette, you are named Jennifer," the woman explained. *That's a weird rule,* Luna thought. She assumed people in the Star

7

Sector did whatever they pleased with their gigantic piles of money. Perhaps the ads she saw posted on wooden billboards were embellished.

"I'm Debbie 3075. We wear name tags with our numbers on them when out in the Star Sector. See look. She pulled out a bright pink name tag from her purse. "Some people even embroider it on their clothes," she continued.

What about people with black or red hair? How about men? Are they Debbies and Jennifers?

"I know redheads tend to be called Julie, but they mostly live in the Cloud Sector," Debbie answered. I don't believe I've seen anyone with black hair in either Sector. "Men don't have assigned names, but if it were up to me, they should be called idiot number one and idiot number two," Debbie joked. Luna let out a curt laugh. This irreverant woman was growing on her.

My name is Luna, by the way. You should come to see us more often.

You should visit me.

"I can take you to some of the best rooftop bars in my city," Debbie bragged. They have amazing views, and you can see all the constellations.

"Am I allowed up there?" Luna inquired shyly.

I don't see why not. Here, take my spare card. Debbie put away the name tag and handed her a silver card. It had a white star on the front and number 3075 on the back. "The key will give you access to the elevators that bring you to the Star Sector," Debbie explained. Just tap the keypad, and it should activate the system.

Luna thanked Debbie and placed the card in her purse. Her chest filled with delight at the opportunity to see the other sectors. Something she could not afford to do on her own.

"Shall we order another round?" Debbie asked. Luna cheered and polished off her drink.

Chapter 2

THE STAR DISTRICT

Luna escorted Debbie into the elevator. After shot number eight, Debbie was struggling to walk, and she knew that Debbie's expensive jewelry made her a target. Luna wanted to ensure her new friend made it home safe and was curious to see the Star Sector. She had only been as high as level twenty, and that was for a class field trip to the Deep-Sea Aquarium. Luna pressed the fifty button and scanned Debbie's key card. When they arrived on the fiftieth floor, they walked into an immaculate white room that reminded her of a doctor's office. The waiting area had a few chairs and vending machines lined up against the wall and bathrooms tucked in the corner.

"I'll be right back, "Debbie announced and rushed into the restroom. A large window with an oak sign that read *Land Sector* was located at the center of the waiting room. Lush viridescent plants encircled the sign, and pink flowers protruded between the large leaves. Several vases with ornate artwork were painted on the side, and pink roses decorated the room. Luna climbed onto one of the wooden benches and peered out the window.

The desolate sidewalks were lined with street lights and pink trees. *I wonder if those are cherry blossoms,* Luna reflected on a landscaping textbook she read. She wished she could pick one of the delicate flowers and show it to Safari. Luna scanned the waiting room and noted no one was nearby. She unlocked the window and opened it. Luna was greeted by fresh air that raked past her cheeks and hair. The sensation was heavenly. Luna finally understood why people who had moved to the Land Sector never returned. Some of her successful high school classmates came to mind, and she wondered where they lived. If she could visit them. A voice interrupted her train of thought.

What are you doing? Luna turned around and was greeted by Debbie. She quickly shut the window.

"I was feeling a bit nauseous and thought some fresh air might help," she lied. Debbie hiccupped and approached the elevator. Green banners with the Land Sector's sigil hung next to the metal doors. Luna admired the gnarled trees in the center of the banner before following Debbie into the elevator.

The next elevator was much nicer and cleaner than the one she was used to riding. The walls were made of plexiglass, and the floor was made of amethyst stone. As they ascended, she took in the beauty of the Land Sector. The trees were in different shades of green, yellow, red, and orange. Vehicles zoomed along highways, and houses were spread as far as the eye could see. Some of the houses even had swimming pools. She saw pictures of these things in magazines. However, it was a completely different experience seeing it in person. She imagined diving into the turquoise pool and how the water contrasted the cold, indigo water of the ocean. Luna began to feel queasy as the objects started to shrink and move farther and farther away. She had never been this high up. Luna closed her eyes and took a deep breath as they made their way above the clouds, trying to suppress her nausea.

The next rest area was an elegant room decorated with purple banners and a cloud in the center of it. "I take it we are in the Cloud Sector," Luna noted while looking around. The ceiling was covered with crystal chandeliers, and a divine mural of the heavens was painted on it. The white marble floor gleamed, and an ivory statue was mounted on a gilded water fountain. The statue was of a beautiful woman with a staff pointed towards the ceiling. "Who's that?" Luna inquired, pointing at the statute.

Oh, that's Selene, Greek goddess of the moons and heavens. She's rather a lovely piece of art. "Don't you think?" Debbie explained. Luna smiled, and they made their way into the rest area. The room had manicured plants and comfy leather couches nearby. The walls were made of glass. Luna peered down and could only see a blanket of whispy clouds that drifted across the night sky. It was picturesque, but her stomach fluttered from being unable to see the ground. Luna swiftly made her way back to Debbie.

Debbie's face turned from white to pale green.

"We should probably take a break," Luna advised, leading Debbie to a couch. Debbie plopped down and let out a low groan. Luna filled two cups of water from the water cooler and handed it to Debbie. Debbie violently slurped down her water while Luna gently sipped hers. It was the most delicious and refreshing water Luna had ever tasted. Water from the Ocean Sector always had a copper aftertaste. Debbie burped and threw the cup on the floor. Luna suppressed a judgmental eyeroll and tried her best to maintain her friendly demeanor.

"Do you want to rest her for a bit?" Luna asked, secretly hoping they could explore the Cloud Sector a bit longer.

"No, we only have one more elevator, and I need to get home," Debbie answered, wiping sweat off her forehead. Luna nodded, trying to mask her disappointment, and helped her friend enter the last elevator.

The last elevator was much more spacious and extravagant. Luna touched the diamond stars imprinted on the door after it closed. Its sparkly black floor reminded her of underwater obsidian that she would sometimes see in mid-ocean ridges. It also had a leather bench where patrons could sit, but the most remarkable aspect of the elevator was the glass ceiling. Luna watched in awe as they moved towards the stars in the sky. She tried to imagine what the Star Sector would look like and how lucky the people were to have such a breathtaking view. Suddenly, the elevator began to accelerate violently. Luna's stomach dropped, and she gripped the bench.

"Are we going to crash?" Luna yelped.

Debbie only let out a drunk laugh. Luna watched the numbers on the elevator rapidly fly up. She shut her eyes and braced for impact. A light ding chimed, and the elevator came to a swift stop. Luna opened her eyes, feeling stupid for panicking.

"You, okay?" Debbie said, letting out a nasally laugh.

"Yeah, just not what I was expecting, " Luna admitted.

Luna walked into a room that reminded her of a Sci-Fi starship she had seen in the movies. Large panel windows displayed outer space, and glowing star lanterns hung from the ceiling. Spaceships and robots roamed around huge skyscrapers. Strange and whimsical holograms repeated advertisements for beauty products, movies, and food. Luna was fascinated and slightly overstimulated by the hypnotic lights. She closed her eyes and took a mental picture. She tried to imagine Safari and Darnelle next to her, taking in the fantastic view.

Luna then turned her attention to the room. In the center was a welcome desk with two ladies in white dresses and a headset. Their faces looked similar to Debbie's, stiff and expressionless. The welcome desk had several small monitors and a control panel with an array of rainbow-colored buttons. White banners with a black star in the center of them were displayed next to the desk. Luna watched Debbie confidently stroll up to the counter.

"Floor 152," she drunkenly yelled to the lady at the counter and handed her the key card. The lady with the number 2675 embroidered on her dress took the it and flashed Debbie an irritated look. The other desk attendant eyed Luna suspiciously. Her long brown hair covered her name tag, so Luna couldn't see the number. Debbie then projected vomited on the floor. Both desk ladies recoiled in disgust and covered their noses. The wall on the right side of the room began to ripple and shift like a Rubix cube. A small section of the wall opened, and a tubular robot with black scrub brushes exited out of a circular shaft. The robot let out soft beeps and vacuumed up Debbie's vomit.

It was black and white in color and had the words Goddard 3450 painted on it. Luna was stunned into silence as the robot slowly rolled back into the wall. That was the last thing she expected to see. One of the desk ladies cleared her throat, and Luna redirected her attention to the front desk. She rushed over next to Debbie and wrapped her arms around her friend, who was struggling to stand.

I'll make sure she gets home safe. "Sorry about the mess," Luna apologized. The desk lady motioned and handed the key card back to Luna. "Come on, Debbie, we are almost home," Luna soothed, guiding her towards the exit.

Chapter 3

VIOLET STRANGERS

Alan dried his eyes and blew his nose with a crumpled-up tissue. His face was sore and swollen from crying. The humiliating scene of Jenny rejecting him replayed over and over in his head. Alan felt like he could never stop crying and hated himself for it. He visualized his parents' cold expressions for getting upset at something they deemed to be trivial, his brother Logan teasing him relentlessly. He was thankful to be alone and made his way into the bathroom. Alan washed his face and scrutinized his image in the mirror. He detested his overweight body, small eyes, and mousy brown hair. However, he felt powerless to do anything about it. Alan sighed, changed his clothes, and laid back down on the bed. He buried his face into the comforter as fresh tears streaked down his face. A knock echoed through the empty condo, interrupting his pity party. Alan wiped his face and put his glasses back on. He looked over at his nightstand and read 2:45 on the digital clock. As if this night could get any worse, he was going to have to deal with his wine-drunk aunt.

Alan reached the door and activated the security camera app on his phone.

"Open uuuuuupppp," Debbie shouted and waved to the camera.

Alan let out a groan and pulled the door open.

"Hiiiiiii, Alan," Debbie squealed, wrapping her leathery arms around him. Alan cringed as vomit was wiped onto his shirt and guided Aunt Debbie to the chic sofa in the living room. Aunt Debbie laid down on the couch and closed her eyes.

"Do you think she will be alright? " a sweet voice asked from the doorway. Alan looked up. A young woman with black hair and a faded violet dress walked in. She wore heavy makeup, and tiny crescent moons floated around her neckline. Her dark eyes darted around the room, and her mouth was slightly opened in awe.

"I think so," Alan hesitated. I take it you're not a friend from the wine lounge.

The stranger closed her mouth and analyzed Alan from top to bottom. Alan pressed down his disheveled hair and adjusted his glasses. He felt self-conscious, and warmth spread across his cheeks. The stranger's face relaxed, and her glittery cheeks glinted in the dim living room light.

"No, we had a great time in the ballroom," the stranger answered.

"What floor is that?" Alan asked, concern filling his chest.

"You should probably ask her when she gets up," she eluded cryptically and pivoted towards the door.

"Wait, would you like some water?" Alan blurted out. He wanted to punch himself for the awkward outburst.

I mean... I know it's a long way down, but you brought my aunt home safely. *Oh my god, shut up*, Alan scolded himself. His face was now bright red. The stranger paused and glanced at the decorative analog clock in the living room.

"Sure, I'm not in a rush," the stranger answered, impervious to the cumbersome conversation. She drifted across the room and sat in the white leather chair next to Aunt Debbie, who was now fast asleep. Her attention was directed at the window that overlooked the city. Alan admired her bronze skin and shiny curls. *She is really pretty and way nicer than Aunt Debbie's usual ghoulish-looking friends,* Alan thought to himself. His parents' harsh comments about ocean dwellers rang in his head, and he felt slightly uncomfortable. Alan busied himself in the kitchen and filled two glasses of water. He handed one glass to the woman.

"Thank you, my name is Luna, by the way," she said.

"Alan," he answered.

I'm sorry I didn't introduce myself. I just wasn't sure what to expect. I was worried you might not want me here.

"Really, why's that," Alan asked tensely, worried he might have given off the wrong impression.

"Well, as you can tell, I'm from the lower floors," she continued. I know it was risky using her key card, but I wanted to make sure that Debbie got home safely.

"Wait, where were you guys?" Alan questioned. Luna bit her lip and shifted her gaze to the floor.

We were in the Ballroom on floor five. Alan's expression shifted from puzzled to panicked. *How could his aunt be so reckless?* he thought to himself. Luna read his expression and tensed up.

"Would it be best if I leave?" she cried, her voice filled with fear.

"No, no need, " Alan reassured. I'm sure Aunt Debbie requested for you to have access, so you should be good. Luna let out a sigh of relief. "How were you able to get up here anyway," Alan asked. Luna opened a hackneyed purse and held out the key card.

She gave me this. We were just discussed some family issues. "I believe something with her husband and someone named Jennifer," Luna shrugged nonchalantly and looked out of the window.

Alan shut his eyes, suppressing a groan. Not only had his aunt put her life in danger, but she was also spilling the family drama to strangers.

"She has a heart of gold, even though I feel like she gets worked up easily," Luna continued. Alan was taken aback by her positive remarks. No one he knew ever praised Aunt Debbie. Would you like this back? Luna held out the card. Alan knew that he should take it, but a part of him wanted to keep seeing the woman. She was kind and non-judgemental. However, she was from the Ocean Sector, and his parents often dissuaded him from associating with people on lower floors.

Alan grabbed the key card and placed it in his pocket.

It would be best if stay the night, and then I can escort you back down in the morning. "I would hate for there to be a misunderstanding," Alan revealed.

"That's very kind of you," Luna responded and turned her attention to Debbie. I'm not entirely sure she would even remember me at this point.

Alan let out a timid laugh. You have no idea. Aunt Debbie can be a handful sometimes.

Luna peered out of the condo window. A peculiar metal machine perched on the wooden patio caught her interest.

"What's that?" Luna inquired, pointing to a copper tube with several green lenses.

"It's a telescope," Alan affirmed. I take it you've never used one. Luna shook her head. It helps us see objects in space, mainly meteors, that might hit our city. Here I'll show you. Alan led her to the glass door to the patio and opened it. The deck was enclosed in a triangular dome with a manicured garden. Luna was impressed by the vast array of stars and large moon that radiated through the dome panels.

"Do I need a space suit?" she asked sheepishly before stepping onto the wooden porch.

Well, the door's already open, so if we were in space, we would be dead," Alan answered, slightly amused. Luna blinked at him and looked unconvinced. "We'll be fine," he reassured and turned a small lever on the side of the telescope. The lenses shifted in front of the telescope. "Just look through here," he said, pointing to a small hole at the bottom of the tube.

Luna closed one eye and peered through the telescope. "I didn't know stars could be red," she buzzed with excitement. I thought they were all white. Those are red giants.

"They are stars close to death," Alan clarified. Stars can also be blue and orange too. It just depends on the temperature.

What about that swirly thing? "Is that a star?" Luna implored.

Alan shifted the lever to the right, and the lenses fanned over. That's galaxy NGC 1300, it has billions of stars. If you look over towards the left, you can see Saturn, one of the gas giants in our solar system. Alan continued shifting the lever to the left.

"That's amazing," Luna exclaimed. Do you get to see this every day? I'm so jealous.

"It's pretty great," Alan agreed. But my family says I spend too much time staring into space and should put more energy into my accounting classes. "Well, they're missing out, " Luna protested, looking up at him. What's the coolest thing you've seen? Maybe… aliens… Luna grinned.

"No, nothing like that," Alan admitted. I did see a comet one time.

"You think cleaning products are cool, " Luna said with a bewildered expression.

"Not that kind of comet, " Alan laughed. It's like a space snowball. Here I'll show you. Alan walked back into the apartment and pulled out a small textbook from one of the wooden bookshelves. "Here, this is what they look like," he said, pointing to a page in the middle of the textbook.

Luna studied the photo of a blue ball of light in the center of the night sky.

"They orginate from an area called the Oort Cloud, which is past Neptune," Alan continued. They form a tail when they approach the sun because the ice on it starts melting.

"I'm sorry, I'm probably boring you with all these astronomy facts," Alan murmured, rubbing the back of his head.

"Not at all," Luna mused. I didn't even know these things existed.

"Really, you never learned it in school," Alan said.

"Well, there's not really much of a sky to look at where I live," Luna admitted. A dispirited expression crossed her face.

"I'm sure there are lots of cool things where you live," Alan declared, trying to lighten the mood.

"Well, I did see an octopus fight a sperm whale once," Luna shared shyly.

"Can't say I've seen that," Alan admitted.

"Did you plant that garden?" Luna inquired, trying to keep the conversation moving.

No, I have a brown thumb and would probably murder all those plants. Our gardener Quan takes care of them. "He comes every weekend to weed and water the plants," Alan explained.

"Hmm, sounds fancy," she said. Can we get a closer look?

"Yeah...sure," Alan agreed. Luna hopped onto the sandstone pavers that led to the garden. She took in the light scent of the rose bushes and the earthy undertones of the moss growing on a oak tree at the base of the garden. Fireflies floated between long stalks of wildflowers. Luna peered into the small pond next to the magnificent tree. Turtles and tawny goldfish bobbed to the surface. They stretched their arms and fins, expecting a meal.

"Oh my gosh, they're so cute," Luna squeaked. And maybe hungry. Alan reflected on his childhood of feeding the fish with his Uncle John. *The fish food dispenser,* Alan thought and made his way to a wooden mailbox that was full of brown pellets. He scooped up some of the food pellets and placed half of them into Luna's hands. He tossed a few into the pond. The fish went into a frenzy and climbed over each other to devour the pellets.

"Oh no, the poor turtles need a snack, too," Luna giggled and tossed her pellets over to the opposite side of the pond. Alan was drawn to her gentle demeanor. She defied ocean-dwelling stereotypes of being loud and rude. He reminded himself that he needed to keep his distance, and he refocused on the pond. The turtles resurfaced and waved thank you as they gobbled up the pellets. "You have your own paradise here," Luna praised. Thank you. Alan hadn't been to the garden for a few years and felt mildly guilty. He made a mental note to try to visit it more often.

They sat in silence for a while, taking in the serenity of the night. Are you ready to come back inside? Luna nodded and followed him back into the condo. Alan finished explaining his theory about how the moon formed when an alarm went off. The window changed from the void of space into a hologram of a bright blue sky with puffy clouds floating by.

"What happened?" Luna demanded.

"It switches to daytime mode at six am," Alan

explained. We are so high in the atmosphere that we don't really see a sunrise or sunset.

"So, it's probably time for me to leave," Luna observed.

I'm afraid so.

" Thanks for the space tour. Maybe I could give you an ocean one if you felt up to it," she said, her cheeks turning slightly pink.

I'd like that. "Here, we can exchange numbers, " Alan blurted out, pulling out his smartphone. Luna shook her head.

I don't have one. You can send me a paper gram if you like. Luna pulled out a piece of paper and handed it to Alan. "You have to put my name, tube number, and the message here," she instructed. I think you can do it on an app, but I'll have to manually send mine. Alan placed the paper in his pocket, and his stomach did somersault in his elation.

I definitely will.

Alan guided Luna back to the welcome desk. She waved goodbye and made her way to the elevator. Before she made it in, Alan grabbed her hand.

"Wait, you forgot something," he said and placed a card into her palm. Luna looked alarmed but put the key card into her purse.

"Thank you," Luna mouthed and pressed the bottom button. Alan watched the elevator doors close as the alluring stranger disappeared. He made his way back to his aunt's apartment, trying to ignore the angry glares from the welcome desk attendants as he passed. He gripped the paper in his pocket, trying to reassure himself that he had made the right choice and that she was worth seeing again.

Chapter 4

THE AUTHORITIES

Luna lifted her cleaver and sliced off the silvery fish's head. She flung it into the trash can behind her and carefully placed the severed body into a cardboard box. She shifted it down to Safari. Safari sealed the box and stacked it onto a wooden pallet. The evening alarm sounded, and the factory workers made their way out the door. Luna and Safari disinfected their stations and joined the masses in the hallway.

What happened to you last weekend? "I thought that old crone kidnapped you," Safari jest and nudged Luna.

"No, I just wanted to make sure she got home safe," Luna acknowledged. And I met someone.

"Oh, I need details," Safari remarked with a salacious grin. A fat man with an orange beard bumped into Safari.

"Watch where you're going, Sean," he yelled. Luna's cheeks grew rosy, and she opened her mouth in protest. Safari grabbed her hand and pulled her to the front of the line.

26

"You can let him use your old name like that," Luna protested.

"He's just mad I ended things with him," Safari shrugged. Besides, I can't let my best friend get fired over Fire Crotch.

"Fire crotch?" Luna paused.

Safari smirked.

"You know what, I don't want to know," Luna admitted as they entered the women's locker room.

Luna grabbed a bag full of sliced lemons from her locker and turned on the shower. While showering, she scrubbed her body with the lemons, trying to dissipate the fishy odor from the factory. She then dried off, dressed, and brushed her hair while sitting on one of the blue locker room benches. Safari joined her, drying her long braids.

"So, what's it like up there?" Safari asked. Did you meet E.T.?

"It was beautiful but very dangerous." "I was lucky not to get arrested," Luna replied. My favorite was honestly the Land Sector because of all the fresh air and plants. But the Star Sector had the best views.

"Maybe you can bring me up next time," Safari sighed. Down here, it is so boring!

"Down here is not that bad; the people here are amazing, and we have the ballroom," Luna protested.

"You think Fire Crotch is amazing?" Safari sneered, crossing her arms.

No…but you know what I mean. "They're weird up there." "They all have the same name, and they put whale jizz on their face." "Kinda culty if you ask me," Luna said.

"Well, they are hella rich, so maybe you could get you a sugar daddy," Safari replied.

"Yeah, I don't think I'm their type, " Luna defended.

Here, let me rephrase that. "I'll get a sugar daddy then," Safari shot back. I'm not sure about the whole whale jizz thing, tho that is kinda weird.

"So, who did you meet up there?" Safari grinned.

No one really, there was some guy staying with Debbie. Safari raised her eyebrows.

I guess she likes them young.

"It wasn't like that," Luna retorted, shaking her head. I think he was like a family member. "Anyway, he was very nice and showed me planets and stuff," Luna trailed off, twirling her hair.

"You like him," Safari teased.

I just met him, but he was a little cute. Besides, it's not like I'll ever see him again.

"Hey, you never know," Safari pointed out and checked her watch. Sorry, girl, it's time for me to go. Luna gave her a hug and waved goodbye.

Luna took out her sketchbook and began to draw the stars and planets she witnessed in the Star Sector. She was in no rush to go back home to the third floor. Even though the factory didn't seem like a great place to stay, it was at least clean. Her mother's apartment was full of roaches, and the pipes would occasionally back up with sewage. She kept the place immaculate, but the infestation was deep within the crumbling walls of the apartment complex. Luna tried her best to remember the celestial objects that she saw in the telescope. She wanted to remember the night sky forever.

Luna continued to work until everyone left the locker room. She searched around, making sure no one was left. Luna sat back on the blue benches and studied the key card Alan handed her. She smiled at the thought of Alan. He's really sweet and reminded her of a giant teddy bear with glasses. She felt sad at the possibility of never seeing him again. It wasn't likely he would want to affiliate with someone with low standing, such as herself. She tucked the key card at the front of the sketchbook. She continued to outline the majestic comet Alan showed her in the astronomy textbook.

After completing the red swirl on Jupiter that resembled an evil eye, Luna checked the digital clock above the doorway. She hastily started gathering her belongings and ran out of the locker room. She had only fifteen minutes before the gates locked. She made her way into the empty hallway. The sound of her footsteps echoed on the white cement walls. The door at the end of the hallway swung open. A scrawny man with gray hair and two police officers emerged from the room. Luna slowed her pace and shifted her gaze to the white tile floor.

"Miss Brooks, how are we doing this evening?" the scrawny man greeted her, light reflecting off his oversized forehead. The police officers eyed her distrustfully. They sported white uniforms and badges with golden stars.

"Hi, Mr. Watson," Luna squeaked, trying not to shake.

"These nice officers just have a few questions for you," Mr. Watson said. Luna held still and gave the officer to the right a fearful glance. "See, officer, she's harmless; she hardly ever talks," Mr. Watson continued. The officer ignored him, siezed Luna's bag. He ripped open the bag and poured the contents out on the floor.

Luna said nothing and held her breath. The second police officer pulled out the star card Alan gifted her from the sketchbook. He placed it in an evidence bag while the first officer pulled her hands behind her back and put her wrist in handcuffs. The second officer took out a nightstick and bashed it into the left side of her face. Luna fell to the ground and let out a soft whimper. Blood and tears streamed down her face. The first officer lifted her back up and pushed her through the factory exit. Mr. Watson watched them leave in silent satisfaction.

Luna closed her eyes, fighting the urge to pass out. Her face was throbbing, and she was pretty sure her left rib was bruised. She thought about Darnelle and wondered if he felt just as scared when he was arrested. The police officer came in with a file and tossed it on the table in front of her.

"Why do you have a key card that is not assigned to you?" he grunted, filling out a pile of documents.

You steal it?

"I wanted to make sure Debbie got home safe. She was from Floor 152, and she was past curfew," Luna uttered. I helped her get the apartment, and her nephew took over. When I got into the elevator, he handed me that card.

"What made him do that?" the police officer continued, not looking up from his paperwork.

I think he made a mistake. "I was really tired, so I didn't look at it and put it in my purse," Luna lied. She didn't want to disclose Alan's involvement.

"You're aware that's a class two misdemeanor," he remarked.

"Yes, but it was a genuine mistake, honest," Luna pleaded.

"So, you are looking at a five thousand dollar fine, and you are restricted to floor six," he sniffed, unphased by her desperate pleas. He pushed the papers and a pen towards her. Sign here. Luna signed and pushed the papers back.

"I...I don't have five thousand," Luna croaked, panic rising in her voice.

"Oh, don't worry, we can arrange something, " the officer remarked dismissively. He gathered up the papers, shoving them in an orange file. Fresh tears streamed down Luna's face as she watched him walk out the windowless room.

Chapter 5

THE PAPER GRAM

Alan studied the address scribbled on the paper that Luna handed him last weekend. He activated his phone and scrolled through several apps. He downloaded the Ocean Sector Message app and typed in Luna's tube number into the search bar. A third-floor location popped up, and a message box appeared on the screen. He paused, unsure of what to send her. *Hey, remember that random guy you met when you dropped off his wine-drunk aunt? Yeah, he wants to meet up with you,* Alan thought. No way he was typing that in. He hadn't heard from Luna in a few days and was hoping she would be able to visit again using Aunt Debbie's card. However, nothing happened. He was nervous about messaging her. On one hand, it was socially frowned upon for him to talk to someone from the lower floors. He could imagine his parents' panic regarding the potential scandal. He also never had much luck with talking to people, let alone girls. However, he couldn't stop thinking about her warm smile and calm demeanor. She was also interested in space, which was a rare quality in anyone he knew. He wanted to at least be friends.

A soft knock came from his aunt's condo door.

"Can you answer it, Alllaan?" Aunt Debbie slurred from the other bedroom. Alan let out an annoyed sigh and opened the security app. A Star Sector police officer appeared on his phone screen. Alan's stomach dropped, and his heart began to race. He wondered if the police already found out about the key card.

He took in a deep breath and tried to relax his face as he opened the door.

"Good afternoon, officer," Alan sputtered.

"Afternoon, son," the officer replied and tilted his sunglasses. He pulled out his badge and held it up to Alan. "SPD, can I come in?" "I have a couple of questions for a Mrs. White," he boomed.

"Yes, of course," Alan agreed and led the police officer to the living room. "I'm Alan Smith, Mrs. White's nephew," Alan continued. "My aunt isn't feeling well, but I can answer any questions you have.

"It's important I talk to her," the officer pressed. We had a serious security breach in the Star Sector. A bottom feeder used your aunt's key card without permission. Alan pressed his lips together at the slur the officer used but said nothing.

"I'll go get her," Alan mumbled and set foot into his aunt's room.

Aunt Debbie was lying in bed holding a glass of white wine. She was watching her favorite soap opera on a hologram screen, and five empty wine glasses rested on her nightstand.

"Is it Harold?" she hiccupped. He's not supposed to see me till next week.

"No, it's an officer asking about your key card," Alan informed her, motioning towards the living room.

"Tell him I'll be out there soon," Aunt Debbie replied. Alan made his way back to the living room and shut the bedroom door behind him.

"She will be out soon," he told the officer. The officer nodded and pulled out a yellow file and a notepad from his briefcase.

"Did anyone out of the ordinary visit you last Saturday?" the officer queried.

"Yes, there was a nice woman who helped my aunt arrive home safely after curfew," Alan answered.

Do you know her name?

Luna, I think.

What time did they arrive?

At about 2:30. The officer began writing on his notepad after each question. Aunt Debbie stubbled into the room and plopped down next them.

"So nice of you to join us," Aunt Debbie said, struggling to focus on the officer. The officer wrinkled his nose from the aroma of stale wine that she permeated.

"I just have a few questions regarding your key card, " the officer notified her. Did you give anyone access to your key card last Saturday, May 31? Alan swallowed hard and watched his aunt.

"Why yesssssss," Aunt Debbie tittered. There was a girl from the fifth floor that helped me get home. "It gets dangerous out there for a beautiful woman such as myself." Aunt Debbie winked and placed her hand on the officer's leg. Alan was mortified. The officer shifted his legs away and continued his investigation.

Did she give you her key card back?

No, but I didn't ask for it. "I think she wouldn't have been able to make it back down," Aunt Debbie answered.

Are you aware that she needs to be registered before giving her access to your card?

"Oh, come on, Jerry," Debbie groaned. It was two in the morning. She was harmless. Besides, I've seen some of your boys bring lots of lovely ladies up without clearance. "We always look the other way because you always keep us safe," Debbie implied with a sly expression. The officer's ears turned crimson. I assure you. She probably didn't know that she was supposed to turn the card in. I mean, she is just a dumb bottom feeder anyway. I promise I'll be more careful.

"It sounds like a simple misunderstanding," the officer suggested, rapidly pushing the papers and notebook back into the briefcase. Alan was amazed by how his aunt slithered out of the dire situation. The officer handed her the key card. Be careful out there, Debbie. He promptly made his way out of the condo, slamming the door behind him.

"You made me get out of bed for that," Aunt Debbie whined.

"I was just trying to help," Alan professed.

"Well, you can help me by getting me more wine," she

said and made her way back into her room. Alan opened the Goddard App on his phone and sent the request to Goddard 345. A miniature robot with six wheels rolled from the kitchen to the bedroom, carrying a wine glass. Alan walked back to his computer desk and reopened the messaging app. He felt liable for getting Luna in trouble. He was going to have to be more careful.

Hi Luna, I hope all is well. Again, thank you for helping my Aunt Debbie. Please let me know if you would like to visit us again to look at the telescope or to meet up for coffee. Take care.

- Alan

Alan read over the message five times before pressing send. He hid Luna's contact information in the astronomy textbook on his bookshelf.

***

Luna flinched as she brought the ice pack to her inflamed face and opened the mailbox on the basement floor. She pulled out a massive stack of envelopes and locked the box with a copper key. She slowly made her way up the staircase, carefully avoiding puddles of urine and trash. She slipped into her mother's apartment and promptly locked the door.

She placed the envelopes on the kitchen counter and looked through them. Most were overdue bills and cheesy magazine ads, but a paper gram from the Star Sector was on the bottom of the stack. The envelope was ivory and had gilded flowers around the edges. On the back was a wax seal with the impression of a star. Luna cautiously opened the envelope and read the message. She was excited to hear from Alan.

Luna put her ice pack back into the freezer and then lifted the lid to a small cardboard box on the kitchen counter. She jumped back as a roach scurried from behind the box onto the counter. She grabbed the roach repellant from under the sink and killed it in one swift spray. Luna cleaned the area and pulled out a brown envelope from the box. It looked so plain and homely compared to the paper gram she received from Alan. She thought she could use her artistic ability to make it look nicer. Luna pulled out her watercolors and paintbrush from underneath the sink and began to decorate the envelope. While she was painting a serene underwater scene, she tried to brainstorm the best way to respond to his letter. She didn't want to reject his invitation or ignore him, but she couldn't see him with the temporary restriction.

After she finished the goldfish at the corner of the envelope, she placed it to the side to dry. She then grabbed a brown paper card and wrote her message.

Hi Alan, thank you for the lovely invitation. I hope you and Aunt Debbie are doing well. I would love to see you again. Drinking coffee and looking up at the stars sounds terrific. Unfortunately, I got injured recently and won't be able to leave the Ocean Sector for a few weeks. However, we can still send each other paper grams. I would love to learn more about space, specifically the swirly stars in the sky you showed me. I have attached a picture of some cool starfish seen from floor seven. Let me know if there is anything else you would like to learn about. Best wishes.

-Luna

Luna added the magazine clip of the starfish and placed both items in the envelope. She carefully copied Alan's tube number from the paper gram she received and sealed it. She jogged back down the stairs and placed it into the basement mail shoot. She was eager to hear back from him, and the excitement she felt distracted her from her bruised face. When she returned to the apartment, she noticed the door was unlocked. All the wind was knocked out of her sails. She knew Mom was home. Luna cautiously crept into the apartment and closed the door.

"Hi, mom," Luna greeted, inching towards the living room. Her mother was in a black dress and smoking a cigarette. Her hair was in disarray, and Luna could tell she was in a horrible mood.

"What's this?" she grunted while studying Alan's message.

"A paper gram from someone I met," Luna answered, trying to keep her voice even. She could tell that her mom was mad, but she knew better than to lie. Dread filled her stomach.

Her mother took another drag from her cigarette and tossed the paper back on the counter. "Staying out of trouble, I hope," she drawled, holding Luna's gaze. Luna looked away.

Just talking and making friends.

"Oh really, did your new friend do that to your face," her mother snarled, squinting her eyes.

"No, just the authorities," Luna replied.

How much do I owe?

"Nothing, we were able to work something out," Luna shifted uncomfortably. Her mother nodded sympathetically.

Well, you shouldn't be talking to them. "They aren't like us," her mother scolded, pouring a glass of cheap whiskey. It's not safe.

"I know," Luna agreed, keeping her eyes on the rust-stained floor.

Her mother finished the shot of whisky and pulled her daughter in a tight embrace.

"I know I'm very hard on you sometimes. I just want to protect you," her mother's voice cracked with emotion. Luna's face filled with sorrow. "I can't lose you too. I've already lost Darnelle to them," her mother whispered. The people I meant aren't like them.

"They are really nice," Luna protested. Her mother shook her head. Doesn't matter if they're nice. The system will always protect them. "Do their dirty work.

You'll understand one day," her mother uttered and slinked towards the bedroom.

Good night, Mom. Her mother lazily waved and closed the door. Luna tucked the letter under her pillow on the living room couch. She pulled the handmade blue quilt from her childhood over her body. Luna closed her eyes and dissolved the tattered apartment. She replaced it with the peaceful garden in the Star Sector.

Chapter 6

STAR LAW

Alan finished reading over the thin paper gram and placed it back into the ocean-themed envelope. He was disappointed that he wouldn't be able to see Luna and had a creeping suspicion that it had to do with the private investigator who visited them a few weeks ago. His thoughts were interrupted by a loud knock on his bedroom door. He placed the envelope in a textbook and pulled open the door.

A man with gray hair and a tuxedo stood in the doorway.

Alan, we are going to be late. "We can't keep your mom waiting," the man said, haphazardly scrolling on the hologram screen of his watch.

"I thought dinner was next week," Alan mumbled.

It was, but your mother insisted that the season is changing, and we need to make a good impression. Pointless trend if you ask me. "You look horrible, by the way," he stated, glancing up at his watch. You should wear something else. Alan dreaded these fancy dinner parties with his family. His parents usually complained the entire time, or his aunt would get drunk with wine and loudly gossip about the other floor

42

residents. He also had to spend hours hearing his brother Logan brag about his latest star coin scam. Alan would rather stay in his room and tell his online friends about the new planet he saw in the Artemus solar system. However, keeping face was always important to his family. Alan put on his tuxedo, combed his hair to the side, and adjusted his glasses. He would have to write to Luna later tonight.

Alan and his father made their way down to the condo lobby. They activated their space suits on the screen of their watch. A plastic helmet and space suit extended from the miniature screen and covered their bodies. Alan's father pushed a red button in the decompression chamber to the lobby floor. A metal door slid behind them, and they both exited the complex. A floating limousine with blue rocket boosters levitated before the building's docking station. Alan and his dad floated across the sidewalk and moved into the vehicle. His mother was busy injecting botox into her face, while a mirror that hovered at eye level. His brother was loudly talking to someone on his earpiece about the decrease in star coin stock. He and his father deactivated their space suits. A ringtone from his father's watch resounded, and his father tapped his earpiece to answer the call. Alan attempted to get his family attention with a slight wave, but they ignored him. They were absorbed in their own lives and conversations. Alan sat in somber silence as the vehicle propelled its way into the night sky.

The vehicle flew around the side of a glass hexagon with several mansions located inside of it. The metal doors on the side of the dome opened, and the limousine flew inside. It landed in front of thousands of marble steps that led to an enormous building that was supported by towering marble columns. White banners covered in blue stars hung around the building. Alan and his family exited the limousine and made their way past a marble fountain with a giant rotating globe. The mansion had the number 175 inscribed on one of the stone columns. Alan's mother, flashed an invitation to a man in a teal uniform at the large steel doors of Mrs. Daley's residence.

Mrs. Daley was a cold and highly unpleasant woman. She made it a sport to comment on Alan's weight even though she was the size of a refrigerator. Alan hated her dinner parties the most.

"Smile, my dear," his mother hissed in his ear. We don't want to offend our hostess.

Alan grimaced and then yelped in pain as his mother pinched his arm. He planted a fake smile on his face and escorted her into the opulent building.

Mrs. Daley greeted Alan and his family with a scowl.

Why are you dressed in blue? "The season is fall," she sniffed. You should be in orange.

"My most sincere apologies, Mrs. Daley," his mother cried. We heard that winter was in season, so we thought blue would be the appropriate attire.

44

Mrs. Daley said nothing and turned away in disgust. Mrs. Smith looked as if she were going to faint. His father led her away and tried his best to soothe her by whispering reassurances. Alan wasn't in the mood to deal with his mother's or Mrs. Daley's theatrics. So, he made his way to the beverage table, which held hundreds of champagne glasses stacked in a pyramid. The room was filled with guests in evening attire cordially chatting to each other. Alan weaved around circular tables with sparkling black tablecloths and orange flower centerpieces that contrasted them. An orchestra of robots in the right corner of the room played soft classical music. Holograms and large TV monitors covered the walls. Most of them showed various forms of Renaissance art. Others include the itinerary and guest list for the dinner party.

Alan was promptly handed a glass of bubbling champagne from a beverage robot and approached by two of his Aunt Debbie's old friends.

"How are your classes going, my dear?" one with long white hair. She batted her clumpy fake eyelashes and flashed crooked yellow teeth. Teeth that reminded Alan of scraggly rocks that would wreck ships.

Alan took a sip of his champagne and adjusted his glass, "Fine, thank you for asking Mrs. Trenchfoot.

"Please, call me Marge," Mrs. Trechfoot cooed.

"I heard that we will have a short winter in the Land Sector," the other said. She was short, fat, and had curly gray hair. Mrs. Mullberry was the nicest out of his

45

aunt's friends, but Alan was always grossed out by the moles that peppered her face and neck.

That's great to hear. "There will be a better harvest this year for us," Alan mumbled, scanning the room. He couldn't mentally handle another dull conversation about the weather. To his dismay, he spotted his intoxicated aunt marching towards them, dragging a sweaty, short man with a giant nose behind her.

"Alan," she yelled, pointing her finger towards him and swirling her martini. I must introduce you to someone important. This is Mr. Finnegan. He's an attorney who works closely with your father. I shared with him how much you were struggling with your classes and thought he might be able to give you some advice.

Alan closed his eyes to suppress a sarcastic comment that resounded in his head. Alan was convinced his aunt only paid attention to something if it dealt with wine or money. Everyone knew Mr. Finnegan was a sleazy divorce attorney and only worked with his dad when he was ending his third marriage. Mr. Finnegan raked his hands through his jet-black toupee and held out his hand. Alan shook it and introduced himself. Aunt Debbie noticed her empty glass and went to the closest beverage robot. Mrs. Trenchfoot and Mrs. Mullberry following closely behind.

"She's quite a remarkable lady, isn't she," Mr. Finnegan commented and then shifted his attention back to Alan.

"So, I've heard," Alan sniffed.

So, what issues are you having with your classes?

"Nothing in particular, just trying to finish the year," Alan answered, peering into his glass.

"Doesn't sound like nothing," Mr. Finnegan pointed out.

"Would it be wrong to say that they're boring and I don't want to go to them?" Alan muttered.

Sounds like you're wasting your time and money. You should let your parents know.

"I've tried. They won't hear of it," Alan responded indifferently.

Well, if you are interested in Star Law, let me know. "I'm sure I could convince your father of its value," Mr. Finnegan offered.

Alan immediately perked up. Mr. Finnegan may know how to legally get Luna to the Star Sector. However, he had to choose his words carefully. He knew Mr. Finnegan was a sucker for his aunt and gossip.

"Perhaps I can get your advice regarding some legal issues my aunt might be facing," Alan murmured.

Mr. Finnegan grinned and nodded.

You can't tell my dad either; she's highly embarrassed about the situation, and it's best not to involve him. Mr. Finnegan's eyes and smile widened.

"My lips are sealed," he whispered. Alan explained the situation regarding Luna, his drunk aunt, the key card, and the private investigator.

"Well, your aunt is lucky she didn't get her key card suspended and a hefty fine," Mr. Finnegan noted after Alan finished his story. The Star Sector takes the security of its borders seriously. However, in some ways, it can be a double standard. Star Sector citizens can visit any floor with ease due to their importance and affluence. However, it's nearly impossible for anyone from the lower floors to move up. I'm not sure what possessed your aunt to go to floor five. "That's incredibly dangerous," Mr. Finnegan remarked.

So, is there a way for people to move to the Star Sector?" Alan inquired.

Yes, but it is extremely difficult. There are two main ways that I've seen it done. The first way is to get an occupation in the Star Sector, but you usually must have an impeccable record and five glowing recommendations from Star citizens. The other way is to get a Day Pass, which is about $10,000 dollars, and fill out a 1077, which is a lengthy twenty-four-page document. Alan's heart deflated. "Why do you ask, anyway?" Mr. Finnegan continued lifting his left eyebrow.

"To keep Aunt Debbie out of trouble, of course," Alan lied.

Make sure you stay out of trouble, too. Like I said, Star Sector takes security seriously. You can't trust bottom feeders anyway. "They bring drugs and decrease our property value," Mr. Finnegan said. Alan nodded in agreement to appease Mr. Finnegan, even though he strongly disagreed with him. Luna hardly seemed like a thief or drug dealer.

The orchestra stopped playing as Mrs. Daley arrived at the front of a podium with a microphone.

"Good evening, everyone. We are about to start the first course of our dinner. Please make yourself comfortable in your assigned seats. All the guests politely applauded, and the orchestra resumed playing. Alan thanked Mr. Finnegan for his time and made his way to the seating chart displayed on the right-side wall monitor. He was hesitant about his next move.

Chapter 7

RHINESTONE DRUG DEALERS

"You have to invite him down here," Safari pressed after reading the papergram.

I'm not sure if he would like it," Luna sighed, watching a roach crawl up the peeling palm tree wallpaper. *Where he comes from is wealthy and splendid, which is the opposite of this place.*

"Not here specifically, I was thinking somewhere else in the Ocean Sector," Safari continued. *I hope she's not thinking of Ballroom,* Luna thought, eyeing her friend.

"Ballroom!" Safari announced.

I believe the Ballroom would be too much. He's kind of a shy guy. He only seemed interested in Astronomy when I met him.

"Hmm, one of those learning types," Safari trailed off. *Oh! Maybe he would like the Deep-Sea Aquarium. There are lots of cool animals, and it has a laid-back atmosphere. Listening to Sylvia Earle drone on and on about ocean currents would always mellow me out after smoking.*

"It's not a bad idea, but I lost my clearance, remember," Luna pointed out. Besides, I'll somehow mess it up. I've never had much luck with guys anyway.

"Trust me, he likes you. You got to at least try," Safari protested. Maybe you should give him head under the table. I'm sure he'll like you even more after that.

Luna rolled her eyes but let out a small laugh. She knew deep down Safari was trying to help, but seeing someone from a wealthier district was risky. She didn't want to get him in trouble.

Luna left the couch and grabbed an envelope, pen, and paper off the kitchen counter. She sat back down and placed the items on her lap.

"What should I say?" Luna asked.

"So, you gotta start with how hot you think his body is. "Guys love that," Safari answered.

"That sounds more like you than me," Luna giggled and began writing.

Hi Alan, would you be interested in going to live music on floor five this weekend? I would love to see you. I also saw a family of dolphins on floor six, which is rare but exciting. Here is an excellent article on bottlenose dolphins I got from the Deep-Sea Aquarium, and you might find it as interesting as I did.Anyway, I hope to hear from you soon. Best wishes

-Luna

"Wow, that article on dolphins is really going to seduce him," Safari asserted in a sarcastic tone.

"I think it's perfectly fine," Luna responded and sealed the letter. Can you hand me my watercolors?

Safari handed her a paintbrush, and they both delicately painted ocean waves on the envelope.

Luna anxiously pulled black hair over her injured eye as she waited in front of the elevator door. Loud rock music reverberated into the humid room, and red lights poured out from the colossal dance hall. People in black leather pooled around her and chatted excitedly about the upcoming show. The elevator let out a soft chime, and Alan walked out in a tuxedo. Luna frowned and quickly pulled Alan to the side to avoid the immense surge of people. His expensive clothes would make him a target.

"I'm so glad you made it. How was the trip?" Luna yelled over the loud music.

Great, not too long. "I take it I wore the wrong stuff for the show," Alan noted, watching the stream of people wearing black combat boots and band t-shirts.

No worries, it's an easy fix. At least you wore black.

Luna pulled off his jacket and bow tie. She placed both items on a trash can and ruffled his hair. It gets pretty hot in there with the huge crowd, so you will be more comfortable. I also doubt anyone will mess with your clothes, so we can pick them up on the way back. I'm also sorry about not telling you what type of show it was. "I'm sorry, I'm babbling," Luna apologized. Alan opened his mouth to respond. "Let's go inside," Luna interrupted and pulled him towards the crowd. Luna felt self-conscious. *How am I already bombing this?* she thought to herself.

The people rushed towards the stage the second the band walked out. The main singer was blindfolded and had several bald spots sprinkled over his head. The lead guitarist had burns all over his face and sported a guitar with spikes on the side. The other band members were covered in lumps and cancerous overgrowth.

They must be from floor one, Luna concluded. *Looks like the radiation is getting worse down there.* The lead singer grabbed the microphone and let out a powerful, animalistic scream. The drummer rapidly started smashing her metal trash cans while fire exploded from the blood-stained guitar. The crowd began to chant and banged large, iron totems decorated with Halloween masks. Luna felt Alan tense up. She realized the scene was probably overwhelming, and it would be best to take him somewhere else.

Luna wrapped her arm around his and flashed him a reassuring look. She led him to the vibrant bar and grabbed the last two seats at the end.

"So, what do you want to drink?" Luna asked while twirling her dragon earrings.

I usually have a glass of wine with my family.

"Let me rephrase my question, do you like beer or whiskey?" Luna continued.

"Umm, maybe beer would be best," Alan answered. Luna signaled at Beatrice. Beatrice swayed across the bar in a long, black dress with a ruby necklace and red-tipped nails.

Always good to see you, my dear. "What can I get you?" Beatrice asked, studying Alan.

"Two draft beers, please," Luna yelled.

Beatrice nodded, winked, and glided away.

Luna took a deep breath, trying her best to calm her nerves. Alan shifted and readjusted his glasses. An awkward silence hung between them. Luna was hesitant about how to break the ice. A sandbar shark swam past one of the portholes and grabbed her attention.

"Hey, let's check the windows while we wait for our drinks. "Maybe we will see a vampire squid tonight," Luna motioned towards the portholes. Sometimes, they swarm when they throw fish out of the fourth floor.

Luna and Alan peered out of the porthole.

"Are those volcanoes?" Alan inquired, furrowing his brow.

So, those are actually hydrothermal vents. The smoke you see coming out of them is filled with minerals like sulfide. I've read they are like hot springs in the Land Sector. "Have you ever been to a hot spring?" Luna asked.

"Yes, my aunts like to go to Yellow Stone Resorts to rejuvenate their skin" Alan answered. I personally don't use them.

Sounds heavenly.

"Maybe we could go there one day," Luna trailed off.

"Y'all seen the colossal squid yet," an animated voice boomed behind them.

Luna and Alan turned around. A man with a hot pink vest and matching chaps flashed them a wide grin. Alan noticed that the man had his bare butt cheeks hanging out of the chaps and looked away in horror.

"Hoodi," Luna uttered in disbelief. The man adjusted his bedazzled rhinestone hat.

In the flesh. What are y'all doing hanging around here? Y'all are missing the party.

"We were just-" Luna started.

"You should join us," Hoodi interrupted and motioned towards the crowd.

Alan paused and studied the man with a perplexed expression. Of course... Sure..." We would be honored," Alan sputtered and followed the eccentric man into the horde of people.

Beatrice approached them with their drinks and raised her eyebrows in surprise. As Luna walked past, she gave Beatrice a pensive look.

Hoodi led them past a midnight blue curtain in the back of the venue. Copper-rusted benches were sprinkled all around the dimly lit room, with people sprawled across them. The people inhaled green smoke out of a tube that was connected to a metallic owl in the center of the table. The owl's green eyes glowed menacingly towards them. Its wings were out stretched in mid-flight. Green smoke occasionally oscillated from vents located on its abdomen. As the people continued to inhale the green gas, they gradually slipped into a deep slumber. Luna's stomach churned in apprehension. She was hesitant as to why such a notorious drug lord like Hoodi would be interested in them.

Hoodi sat down and signaled for them to do the same. He began inhaling the smoke and blew it out of his nose, studying them closely.

"You want a hit," he finally asked, holding out the metal tube.

Alan grabbed the tube and examined it.

What is it?

Hoodi inhaled more smoke and blew out miniature rings.

"Vapor, some people call it Quartz," he answered. It mellows you out. Try some.

Alan looked over at Luna for approval. Luna shrugged and pressed her lips together. Alan apprehensively inhaled the peculiar gas. It tasted like bubble gum but burned his throat and nose. He started violently coughing and handed the metal tube back to Hoodi. Hoodi let out a laugh and motioned it towards Luna.

"No, thank you," Luna politely declined and pushed the tube back to Hoodi.

"Here, take it," he commanded, the friendly tone edging towards aggression. Luna decided it would be best to go along with Hoodi. She was warned to either stay on his good side or out of his way. Luna took the tube, inhaled, and quickly handed it back. Luna began to feel slow as time passed, and her body sank into the chair. She sat up, trying to fight off sleep, and stretched her arms.

You know, I just put in an order for drinks.

"Would you be so kind as to pick it up for us?" Hoodi asked, staring intensely at Luna.

Luna shifted uncomfortably, unsure if it would be best to leave Alan alone with him. Hoodi seemed to read her mind.

Don't worry, don't worry. He won't be alone. I'll be here to keep him company. Now… "Go ahead and pick up that drink order for me," Hoodi pressed.

Luna noticed three men wearing all black and a mask with a pink triangle standing in the doorway. Probably some of Hoodi's henchmen. Luna realized she didn't have much of a choice. She sighed and smiled towards Alan, trying her best to pretend nothing was amiss. She tenderly placed her hand on his and whispered. I'll be back in five. Don't move a muscle. Luna slid off the booth and made her way towards Beatrice.

***

Alan watched Luna sway towards the door and out of the room. He felt eerily calm, and his thoughts were slow and hazy. The Ocean Sector sigil, a light blue swirl next to Hoodi, began to move. The hallucination startled Alan, and he brought his attention back to Hoodi.

"She's pretty," Hoodi commented. Where did y'all meet? Smoke swirling around his clean-shaven face. Alan blinked, hesitant about what to say. He decided to be honest with the odd man.

"My aunt brought her home one night," Alan answered.

Hmmm, kinda freaky, but no judgment here. You must be very close to your family.

"No, not like that," Alan gasped in astonishment. My aunt sometimes needs help getting home after a few drinks. And I rent a room from my aunt. "Luna was just making sure she got home safe, and we kinda ran into each other," Alan fumbled, his words slightly slurring.

Hoodi held out his hand and chuckled.

I know what you mean, silly. I was only teasing. More importantly, where does your aunt live?

"Star Sector," Alan replied and felt instantaneously stupid for oversharing. His thoughts were swimming and fading in and out.

Hoodi raised his eyebrows in surprise. "Really, is that so?" he drawled, taking another drag of the vapor. So, are you two together? Hoodi's eyes narrowed, motioning towards the ballroom.

"It's not like that. We are just friends," Alan winced, panic rising to his chest.

Hoodi roared with laughter, smoke overflowing from his mouth like a dragon.

Lies!

No one comes from the Star Sector to this place over some friends.

Alan sat in silence, contemplating his own feelings and motives.

"I'm just kidding," Hoodi said light-heartedly and placed his hand on Alan's shoulder. You think you're the first guy that has come down here over some girl. It's all good. In fact, it explains that walnut-sized black eye. "Did you try to sneak her back up?" Hoodi inquired.

"No, I just gave her my aunt's extra key card," Alan said, remorse creeping up his spine.

"Rookie move," Hoodi commented and scratched his chin. The authorities have tracking devices on those and can be real Debbie Downers when they are with the wrong person. Hence, your lady's swollen face. I'm sure, though, with the right moves, you could get her up there.

"Yeah, only a couple grand," Alan murmured.

A grin crept across Hoodi's face, flashing yellow cigarette-stained teeth. See, that's where I step in.

What do you mean?

Hoodi's grin widened. Well, I am all about making a profit. I'm what they call a business manager of street pharmacists.

"That's a fancy way of calling yourself a drug lord," Alan replied and took in another puff.

"Drug lord has such a negative connotation; hence, business manager sounds more professional," Hoodi said. I am very good at making a lot of money very quickly, which is what you need to get her up there. Correct?

Alan said nothing and inhaled more smoke.

You also seem comfortable with Vapor, so what's the hold-up?

"My brother Logan would take hits of stardust all the time in high school, so I've seen stuff like this before," Alan uttered. Besides, smoking and selling are two completely different things.

"True, true," Hoodi nodded in agreement. Besides, you rich kids would be bored with Vapor anyway. Have you heard of Gush?

Alan shook his head. Hoodi took out a pill container and removed a rainbow pill from the bottle. He placed it carefully on the table. So, this little guy goes for $200 and is great for a party or night out. My customers say it makes you feel like you won a million dollars. Those rich kids up there would eat it up, and you only have to sell sixty at most. Alan picked up the pill and rolled it around in his hand.

Any side effects?

You might feel nauseous or tired afterward. "Nothing to worry about," Hoodi explained.

Why me?

"Why not you?" Hoodi boomed. You're perfect. No one would suspect you.

Alan continued studying the pill. Hoodi wasn't wrong. No one ever noticed him, not even his family. That's why he liked Luna so much. She didn't make him feel invisible.

"I'm not sure," Alan sighed and handed the rainbow pill back to Hoodi.

I'll tell you what. The first one is on the house. I'll leave you with my contact info, and if you change your mind, just send me a paper gram with the message; *I love rainbows and your initials*. Don't want to alert the authorities.

"That sounds kinda gay," Alan stated without thinking.

"Well, in case you haven't noticed, I'm not entirely straight," Hoodi affirmed, motioning toward his flamboyant outfit.

"Well, you don't sound gay," Alan continued.

"Man, what does gay even sound like?" Hoodi roared in irritation. You need to stop watching Star TV. Anyway, we are getting off-topic. What's important is you take my contact info. Hoodi handed him a pink paper, and Alan shoved it in his pocket. Alan felt silly for the outburst and apologized under his breath.

Hoodi said nothing and continued puffing on the metal tube.

Luna meandered back to their table with a tray of drinks and placed them on the glass table. Hoodi slipped the pill in one of the cups and motioned towards the tray.

"The choice is yours," he said, his blue eyes gleaming in delight. Alan picked up the beverage with the pill in it and passed the other drink to Luna. Hoodi picked up his beverage and winked.

"To good times," Hoodi cheered.

They all tapped glasses together and enjoyed their drinks.

Chapter 8

PROMISES

"What was that about?" Luna inquired as they made their way back to the bar.

"Nothing important," Alan reassured her.

Luna didn't believe him and flashed him a distressed look.

That pill doesn't seem like nothing.

"Just an offer, nothing more," Alan shrugged.

"You have to be careful with Hoodi, he always finds a way of twisting things to get his way," Luna pleaded. I've known a lot of people who have vanished when things don't go right. I just don't want anything to happen to you while you're down here.

Hoodi hardly felt like a threat to Alan. He seemed eccentric but friendly. Alan pulled her in and gave her shoulder a reassuring squeeze.

It was nothing like that. Nothing I haven't seen or can't handle. I'll be fine, I promise. "How is your eye feeling?" he deflected.

It still hurts, but I'll be okay.

What happened?

"The authorities," Luna bristled and sat down at a poorly painted green table at the edge of the stage. A small wax candle burned in the center of the table. Luna redirected her attention back to the stage, trying to calm her nerves. An elaborate dog puppet streamed across the stage around the band members. Several members of the crowd were surfing on top of the sea of people. A few of them were standing on top of the crowd surfers.

"What are they doing?" Alan inquired in confusion.

"Oh yeah, they're surfing a crowd surfer," Luna laughed. The band Canibal Goblins encourages it.

"Looks painful," Alan cringed.

Alan experienced a tingling sensation throughout his body as if he were slightly pricked on the outside of his skin. *It's probably the Gush,* he thought and braced himself. Alan's heart started racing, and euphoria enveloped his body. His surroundings became bright and vibrant. Even the loud, unpleasant music sounded better. Alan felt an intense surge of energy and grabbed Luna's hand.

"Let's go up to the front," he exclaimed, sweat pouring onto his face. Luna peered into his dilated eyes. Worry washed over her. She wanted to protest but didn't have the heart to confront him about Hoodi and the peculiar pills. She instead let him lead her to the front of the stage.

***

Alan awoke, pain radiating from behind his eyes. He was lying on a cloth couch that reeked of mildew. The unpleasant stench sent a wave of nausea to his senses. Alan gagged, and Luna placed a miniature trash bin next to him. Alan vomited into the trash can, and Luna tenderly rubbed his back. Luna held up a cup to his mouth. "Here, drink this. You are probably dehydrated," she breathed. Alan sipped the water and immediately wanted to spit it out. It had an earthy smell and a robust copper aftertaste. Alan forced down some water and handed the cup back to Luna.

Thank you. What happened? "Where am I?" he asked, rubbing his eyes and taking in his surroundings.

"We are at Beatrice's apartment," Luna answered and placed the cup of water onto the concrete floor.

Beatrice?

"Someone called," a deep voice echoed from behind them. A heavy woman with long brown hair towered over the couch. She had large green eyes, and her face was fat like a frog.

"Oh hey, sorry for crashing on your couch," Alan started and rubbed the back of his head.

No need for apologies. "It's past curfew anyways," Beatrice responded, lazily swirling her wine. You won't be able to head back anytime soon. Alan's head began to throb, and he squeezed his eyes shut in pain.

My head is murdering me.

65

"Hmm, what did you take?" Beatrice asked while taking a sip from the glass.

"Gush," Alan answered.

"Ha, that new rainbow pill Hoodi's been going on about it," Beatrice chuckled. You don't strike me as the adventurous type.

"I'm just glad you didn't die," Luna interjected and handed the cup of water to Beatrice. Hoodi can't... he can't be trusted. I know he seems nice, but he's all about making a profit.

"I've heard that some people on floor two overdosed on some Tranq he sold them," Beatrice added and walked into the kitchen.

Tranq?

Alan gave Luna a mystified look.

"Tranq, like tranquilizer from box jellyfish," Luna explained. It's like this magenta fluid taken from these jellyfish congregating around floor seventeen, and people inject it into their bodies. Mostly the arms. Alan recoiled at the idea of needles and jellyfish venom.

"Why do that?" he winced.

Same reason you did. "It makes you really high," Luna responded with a slight laugh. Most people die from infections from the needles, and if you take it for an extended period, it can cause paralysis. Hoodi is one of the leading distributors of Tranq in the Ocean Sector, amongst other things. Did he try to sell you some of that, too?

Alan didn't want to give her the impression that he was into drugs, so he decided to be honest with her about his encounter with Hoodi.

"No, he asked me if I was interested in selling Gush," Alan admitted and placed his hand on top of Luna's hand.

"And you said no, right?" Luna trembled.

I didn't answer ."But I kinda need the money," Alan admitted. I would just do it for a bit, and I could back out when I've sold enough.

Luna pulled her hand away, and her eyes watered. "It isn't worth it," she protested. Please just tell him you're not interested.

Promise!

"Don't worry, I won't answer," Alan said, holding his hands up. He was alarmed by her adverse reaction.

"Good," Luna declared and got up from the couch.

I talked to Beatrice, and she agreed to let you stay here for the night. "I'll be in the room over there if you need me," Luna motioned toward a green wooden door and averted his gaze.

Thanks.

Is there a bathroom I could use?

Luna pointed to the door next to her. I'm going to help Beatrice in the kitchen. Feel free to wash up. It might make you feel better. Luna promptly turned and left him alone.

Alan stumbled into the bathroom and turned on the light. He flinched as a dozen erratic bugs scattered from the brown floor to the cracks in the bathroom wall. The bugs had large antennas and were oval-shaped. Seeing them scurry away made his skin crawl. The sink faucet had rust spots, and there was a red ring around the bottom of the basin, most likely from the hard water. He looked into the small bathroom mirror. He was covered in sweat, and his eyes were bloodshot. No wonder Luna was worried about him. Alan turned on the faucet to wash his face in an attempt to improve his appearance. The faucet made a horrible grinding noise before brown water slashed from the spigot. Alan quickly shut off the faucet in disgust. He decided he could just use his shirt to wipe his face.

Suddenly, the smell of sewage and rot filled his nose. He pulled his shirt over his nose and investigated the room to find the source of the scent. Black goop was foaming up from a drain in front of the toilet. It swirled around and returned to the drain, leaving an inky stain. Alan rushed out of the bathroom and made his way into the kitchen. Luna was pouring hot water into three tea cups. Beatrice was immersed in a magazine and continued to sip her wine.

"Hey, I saw sewage come out of the floor drain in your bathroom," Alan notified them. I think there might be an issue with your plumbing.

"Oh yeah, it happens whenever you turn the sink or shower," Beatrice responded, not looking up from her magazine.

"Oh, sorry, I should have warned you," Luna admitted, giving Alan a sympathetic smile. The sewage backs up anywhere below floor four. When I finish, I'll pour vinegar down the drain to dispel the smell.

That stinks. Why hasn't it been fixed?

"The authorities don't see a need to fix it," Beatrice grumbled. *That's the second time they mentioned the authorities,* Alan thought. Why hadn't he heard of them before? He wanted to find out more.

Who are the authorities?

"They… "Beatrice started.

"I'll explain some other time," Luna interrupted and nudged Beatrice with her elbow. Beatrice shot her an irritated look and continued reading her magazine. Here, try some tea. It should help with the pain and nausea. Luna handed him the teacup and took a huge gulp out of hers. Delight enveloped her face. Alan brought the cup to his mouth. The scent of peppermint and ginger rippled through his nose. He gradually sipped the tea and felt immediate relief. He wanted to ask more questions about the authorities but could sense that Luna didn't want to talk about it. So, he decided to drop the subject.

"Thank you for the tea. It's quite good," Alan remarked, changing the subject. What did you put in here?

"Secret recipe," Luna winked.

Hopefully, no Gush. I don't think I'll make it through the night.

Luna giggled, and Beatrice peered up from her magazine in amusement. Alan's chest filled with jubilation. He never experienced this amount of warmth or attention from his own family. They were probably scrolling on their holographic screens, unaware that he was gone. Luna deserved more than this. He made a promise to himself he would better her life just like she mended his tonight.

Chapter 9

DEEP SEA DEALINGS

Alan typed, *I love rainbows*, into the message box. He felt utterly ridiculous but couldn't resist Hoodi's offer. He contemplated the deal for a few weeks. He took in the information Mr. Finnegan shared with him and decided he would get Luna a Day Pass. A part of him felt the need to make up for all the trouble that he and aunt had caused her in the past. Furthermore, his short visit to the Ocean Sector left him traumatized, and he had no desire to go back.

He felt it would be better to share all the amazing things that the Star Sector had to offer instead. The completing the application would be easy. He was used to doing tedious paperwork in his accounting classes. However, the challenging part would be raising the $10,000 dollars. Alan was heavily invested in his accounting classes, so he wasn't able to work and raise the money the honest way. So, selling a few pills seemed easy and to be the best option. Yes, it was underhanded and dangerous. However, he was confident no one would notice or suspect him. Shoot, his brother Logan was high on stardust most of his high school years, and no one batted an eye.

A notification flashed onto the screen with unfamiliar symbols as the contact. Alan opened the message from Hoodi and only saw the characters of a rainbow and a winky face in the chat bubble. *I feel like he's flirting with me,* Alan thought, shaking his head in disbelief. Another message popped up on the screen.

Hoodi: Floor twenty, come see the grand opening of the new Bioluminesce Exhibit in the Deep-Sea Aquarium next weekend.

So, he wants to meet there, Alan concluded.

Alan: *thumbs up*

Hoodi: *sent a heart* Bringing a friend.

The first person that came to mind was Luna. However, she was against him talking to Hoodi, so he would have to be discreet while he made his exchange. He hated being dishonest but was confident she would never find out. Alan tapped his watch, and the search engine appeared in the hologram. He researched a map of the Deep-Sea Aquarium and information regarding the new exhibit. The map showed a long hallway leading to the bathrooms and connected to the Phytoplankton exhibit. Hoodi could hide the pills in that bathroom. He could excuse himself and then grab them later. He sent Hoodi a screenshot of the section of the map.

Alan: "How about we meet between the new exhibit and then go to the Phytoplankton section?

He added a red circle in front of the restroom. Alan held his breath and hoped Hoodi would understand.

Hoodi: * *sent a smiley face with glasses* * We can meet up at 1 pm in 3. Make sure not to eat anything that might upset your stomach.

So, he would drop it off at one in the afternoon, and it would be in the third stall of the bathroom.

Alan: *sent him a thumbs up*

This was a lot easier than he was expecting. Selling would be more challenging.

Hoodi: See you soon.

Alan closed the application. He found it a little suspicious that Hoodi was able to message back on his phone. Maybe Hoodi didn't live in the Ocean Sector but only sold down there. Luna's warning echoed in his head. He promptly ignored it, pulled open Luna's contact information, and sent her an invitation. He desperately hoped she would agree to come with him.

***

"I don't know, what do you think?" Luna asked and showed Beatrice the paper gram. Beatrice held her coffee mug up to her lips and scanned the paper.

Doesn't matter what I think, do you want to go?

I'm not sure, that's why I asked you.

Beatrice said nothing and made her way to the refrigerator.

"Do you like him?" Luna voiced weakly. She wanted Beatrice to like her new friend, but she could sense Beatrice's wariness.

I'm not sure. He seemed nice, but he's not very sharp. "I mean, honestly, who takes drugs from Hoodi," Beatrice sniffed.

"I think he just doesn't understand how things work down here," Luna defended. I mean, did you see his expression when the sewage backed up? I still feel embarrassed about it.

Beatrice shrugged.

It wasn't that bad. He still wants to come back. The more important thing is, do you like him?

Luna grabbed onto her right arm and averted her gaze.

Yes, as a person, he's really cool. I'm just not too crazy about the drugs. But… I also really want to see the aquarium. They have a new exhibit.

"Did you get your clearance back?" Beatrice questioned.

Yes, they finally lifted it.

Then you already know. Luna hugged Beatrice and was glad she consulted her friend. She rushed back to her mother's apartment.

Luna inspected her reflection in the dusty mirror. She pulled her hair back with a blue butterfly clip her mother gifted her on her birthday. She added blue glitter to her cheekbones and wore a necklace with tiny sea turtles and matching earrings. She changed her nail color to sky blue, and Safari let her borrow a matching romper. Luna was silently hoping she looked nice for Alan.

As she made her way out of the apartment, she felt excited to visit the Deep-Sea Aquarium but nervous to see Alan again. She was anticipating a better time than their encounter with Hoodi. Luna crawled through the plastic transportation tubes into the elevator room. Moving through them always made her uneasy due to the horror stories she heard about tubes bursting from age, but they were the only way to move between buildings in the Ocean Sector. A manta ray cast a shadow over her as it glided between the buildings. *I wonder why it came this deep,* Luna pondered. *I hope there isn't an issue with the food supply again.* She pushed the 15 button and scanned her blue key card.

Luna promptly arrived at the level fifth teen. She walked into an immense glass room. Humpback whales swarmed around the glass dome, blowing bubbles. Many families were milling about the room and taking pictures. Some divers scraped algae off the outer glass while others waved at the carefree guest. Luna searched the crowd and found Alan standing in front of the ticket booth. He was dressed in polo and khakis. His hair was combed to the side, and he wore a shy smile. He looked strikingly handsome, and Luna's heart fluttered. She gave him a wave and ran over to greet him.

Here's your ticket.

Luna placed the ticket in her pocket and hugged him. She was overjoyed to not only see him but get a free entrance into her favorite park.

Thank you. "You have no idea what this means to me," Luna cheered. She drank in his fresh cologne. Alan patted her on the back, and Luna noticed that several people were staring at them. Luna felt self-conscious and let go.

"I wasn't expecting to see a mob of whales when I got here," Alan commented, looking upward.

Yeah, they're hunting. Really? Yes, they blow little bubbles to create bubble nets with their baleen to catch krill.

Alan nodded in astonishment.

Where should we go first? Alan inquired, holding up the map. Luna was flattered that he would ask for her input.

The Penguin Exhibit is my favorite, but the corals are beautiful this time of year. I also heard from Beatrice that the new Bioluminescent section is legendary. We could buy some pet gulper eels if we get there early enough. What do you think?

We could cover this part of the aquarium first. Alan motioned towards the shallow seas portion of the park. Then we could get lunch, go to the Bioluminescent exhibit, and finish the rest of the park.

Are you up for all that walking? "This aquarium is the largest in the sector," Luna mentioned.

"Don't worry, I wore my tennis shoes," Alan laughed, leading them towards the Coral Reef section.

***

Alan was blown away by all the marine life he encountered in the Deep-Sea Aquarium. In his childhood, some of his parents' wealthy friends had freshwater aquariums, and he saw pictures of some of the animals in textbooks. However, they didn't hold a candle to the diverse array of plants and animals he witnessed in each section of the park. They started at Coral Fields, which contained several tanks of tropical and cold-water corals.

The tropical corals were brightly colored and had several schools of radiant fish that sauntered around vast fields of kelp. Luna pointed to a couple of pink seahorses with their tails interlocked, close to the glass.

"They are holding tails. Isn't that cute," Luna trilled. Did you know when sea horses couple, they stay together for life? "Wouldn't it be wonderful to be a seahorse," she remarked happily.

Alan found the comment to be a little weird but didn't want to offend her.

Hmm, I don't like the idea of having hundreds of babies. "Sounds painful," Alan joked.

Luna giggled and shifted her attention to the cold-water corals. Alan felt a burst of confidence from being able to make her laugh. The cold-water corals contrasted with the tropics. They were gray and brittle starfish slithered over the barren sandy bottom of the tank.

"It looks like a graveyard," Alan commented. "There's life, but it's mostly under the sand," Luna reassured. She pointed to a fire worm dragging its prey into the sand. Sometimes, things aren't as they seem.

Luna and Alan passed a colossal clam shell.

"Oh look, they brought back pearl diving," Luna said and pointed to the shell. The shell was positioned in front of a swimming pool with ropes hanging in it. An aquarium attendant stood inside the shell sorting through diver gear.

Pearls?

"Yeah, you get an oyster on one of the ropes," Luna explained. It sometimes has a pearl and you get to keep it.

"Do you want me to get you one?"Alan volunteered in an attempt to impress Luna.

"Yes, please," Luna grinned. I'll shuck it for you when you come back.

Alan pulled on the orange dive suit. The overworked employee placed an outdated metal helmet on his head. Alan felt constrained and uncomfortable in the dive suit, but he was determined to get an oyster. Luna guided him to the edge of the pool and held up the air tube that connected to the helmet. He wobbled into the pool and let his body sink to the bottom. The water was cold and eerily quiet. He was desperate to get in and out. Alan wrapped his hand around the first oyster he saw and ripped it off the rope. He stuffed it in his pocket and climbed up a ladder connected to the wall of the pool. He flung his body onto the poolside and held up the precious oyster. Luna held the oyster in her hands while Alan struggled out of the suit.

Luna led him to the sink.

"Can you grab one of those shucking knives?" she said while rinsing off the oyster. Thin knives with a wooden handle and rusty blade hung above the sink. Luna cracked the oyster open with ease and pulled the fleshy inside. Alan watched in disgust as she sliced it open and rummaged her fingers through its gooey intestines. Luna pulled out the pearl and rinsed it off. She delicately placed it into Alan's hand. Alan studied the pearl. It was smooth like a marble and had the same coloration as the inside of the oyster's shell. Luna chucked the dead oyster in the trash and washed her hands.

You picked the perfect one. "They usually aren't that even," Luna commented.

Thanks. He attempted to return it to her, but she curled his hand over the pearl.

"Are you sure you don't want to keep it?" Alan persuaded. The extraction process mildly grossed him out.

You dived for it.

"You earned it," Luna proclaimed, leading him towards the penguin enclosure.

Several species of penguins congregated in the icy room. Some of them were small and carried stones to jagged piles of rocks. Others slid down ice banks and splashed around in the water. The emperor penguins, which were the largest, huddled around as a pact and silently judged the other penguins that frolicked around the arctic habitat. Luna shared what she knew about them.

"The Chinstrap penguins are cute, but my favorite is the Gentoo penguins," she informed him while pointing at a penguin with a silver fish in its mouth. I wish we could see them on the lower floors, but they mainly live in the Land Sector around nothing but snow.

It looks like you're quite the penguin expert.

How do you know so much about these animals?

I mostly grew up around them, but I also collected articles about them and put them in my sketchbook.

Would you like to see it?

Sure. Luna pulled out a small, tattered notebook from her purse and handed it to him. The pages were full of magazine clippings and a few plant samples.

"Looks great," Alan complimented and handed it back to her. It reminded him of his Astronomy Blog but on a different subject.

Why study all that?

I would like to be a tour guide here someday, and I want to ensure I can answer everyone's questions. Why not start now?

You seem knowledgeable.

"I can't afford to live here, and the aquarium requires you to live on floor fifteen," Luna explained. So, I mainly just visit. Don't worry, I've been saving up.

So, where do you work then?

"In a Tilapia packaging plant, not as glamorous and kinda smelly," Luna answered.

"At least you're working. I am taking a bunch of boring accounting classes at the moment," Alan noted.

"Blegh, no, thank you," Luna mused.

Why don't you study Astronomy instead?

Alan shook his head. My parents don't consider it to be a real job. "Real jobs only deal with money," Alan echoed his father.

"Maybe you find a way to make money," Luna suggested.

Maybe... Alan checked the time on his watch, desperate to change the conversation topic. It was noon.

Are you hungry?

Yes, you gotta try the sticky buns here. "They are a little expensive but definitely worth it," Luna told him, leading them to the food court at the center of the aquarium.

Luna placed a tray of three sticky buns and a brown dip sauce before Alan. She handed him a pair of wooden chopsticks and sat beside him. The sticky buns sent a mouthwatering aroma that filled Alan's nose. He was ecstatic to try them. Most of the food in the Star Sector was bland or healthy. He dipped one of the sticky buns into the brown sauce. He bit into it, and a whirlwind of spices exploded in his mouth.

"Mmm, that's amazing," he said and stuffed the other two into his mouth.

Luna beamed and consumed hers. There's a noodle shop near where I live that has better buns than these, and I'll take you next time you come down.

What's food like in the Star Sector? Is it all space-themed? I heard you have fabulous freeze-dried food like astronaut ice cream.

"It's okay," Alan said between bites. Not as spicy as this. If you want, I can bring you some astronaut ice cream. You can find it at any docking station where I live.

Please do. "I would eat that ice cream every day," Luna expressed. They finished their meals and made their way to the Bioluminescence Exhibit.

The Bioluminescence section was behind a large curtain and shrouded in darkness. The only light from the room originated from bizarre mushrooms and plants grown in glass jars all around the room. A large tank was on the left side of the room, and the flashes of blue fish hypnotized people. Luna was reading about red copepods on a computer screen when Alan rechecked his watch. *Five minutes till one, I need to go to the bathroom,* Alan noted.

Hey, I'm going to use the restroom. "I'll be right back," Alan whispered in her ear.

Luna nodded, not taking her eyes off the glowing screen.

Alan made his way to the hallway he marked on the map. It was empty because most of the guests were enthralled by the luminous exhibit. As he approached the restroom door, he saw a hooded man with a pink triangle on his sweatshirt exit the bathroom. They briefly made eye contact before Alan entered the bathroom. *That must be one of Hoodi's dealers,* Alan thought, walking into the third stall. He searched around and noticed that one of the tiles behind the flusher was loose. He shook the tile and pulled out a pill container. He frantically placed it in his pocket and put the tile back. He flushed the toilet and washed his hands, hoping he wouldn't draw any attention. Luckily, the bathroom was empty. Alan quickly joined Luna next to the sea angler display. She excitedly held up a bag full of transparent gulper eels.

Chapter 10

PARTY

Alan placed a plastic canister on his wardrobe and activated the bubbler on the top lid. The gulper eel scowled at him, flexing its enormous jaws. Alan opened the lid and threw bits of frozen shrimp. The gulper eel eviscerated the meat and greedily guzzled down the meal in glee. Alan could hardly understand why Luna found the creature to be cute. It reminded him of an undersea hag. However, he didn't want to hurt her feelings by refuse the gift. He pulled out his phone and notified Hoodi that he was able to get the pills. Hoodi sent him a thumbs-up and told him to contact him when he finished selling all of them. Alan pulled out five pills and placed them in a plastic bag. He put the other pills into the bottom of the guest bedroom dresser in his parents' apartment.

He slowly approached to his brother's room, trying to decide how he would convince him to buy in. Alan tapped on the door and waited. Loud music and video game sound effects echoed from the other side.

"Come in," Logan called. Alan opened the door and was greeted by a purple cloud of Quartz. Logan and his friend Cody were heavily invested in a round of virtual football. Cody was a year older than Alan and had copper-red hair. He was an even bigger jerk than his brother Logan. Alan was displeased but not surprised he was over. Logan took a drag from his vape, which resembled a purple flash drive. Cody shoved a handful of Hot Cheetos into his mouth and rinsed it down with Mountain Dew.

"Mom, can you get us some more pizza rolls?" Logan demanded, not taking his eyes off the screen.

It's me, Alan.

Oh sorry. Alan, can you get me some more pizza rolls?

Alan wasn't in the mood to deal with his brother and ignored his request. He sat down next to him. Cody lifted his leg and let out a long, wet fart. Alan wrinkled his nose in disgust.

"Bro, did you just shit yourself," Logan shouted. Dude, go to the bathroom that's disgusting.

Sorry man, my fart just turned into a shart.

"My bad," Cody chuckled.

"Are you guys going out tonight?" Alan asked, adjusting his glasses.

Perhaps. "Why do you care?" Cody sniffed.

Well, I got some stuff you might be interested in and was wondering if you guys wanted to try it with me. It makes you really hype.

Logan put down his controller and narrowed his eyes. Since when did you get into drugs?

I've always done them. "I just like to vibe by myself," Alan lied. It's called Gush. I tried some last week, and I thought you might want in.

Alan pulled out the pills and showed them to Logan and Cody. Cody grabbed one of the pills and popped it into his mouth. He shifted his attention back to the game.

Bro, what the fuck? "You just gonna take random pills that someone just gave you," Logan gasped and shoved his friend.

Chill…It's probably candy. I'll be fine.

Logan pulled out a pill and studied Alan. Alan tried to keep his face still. Logan shrugged and swallowed it. He and Cody started yelling slurs at the players in the game.

"I'll grab some more snacks," Alan told them, desperate to escape the two screeching maniacs. He went to the kitchen and placed a plate of pizza rolls into the microwave. While he was waiting for the pizza roll to heat up, the service bot, Goddard 1, rolled in.

"I could have heated that for you, Master Alan," the golden robot beeped. Goddard was one of five robots that helped keep the house clean and aided the family. The robots were bulky and humanoid in shape. They had multiple arms and large yellow eyes that resembled car lights.

"No need, Goddard," Alan sighed.

"At least let me bring up the tray," Goddard politely chimed.

Maybe you can get a cooler ready and bring up some beers.

As you wish, master. The robot politely bowed and made its way to the next room. Alan strategized that getting his brother intoxicated might increase his chances of getting invited to a party. A party meant more potential sales.

Alan returned and placed the pizza rolls on the table next to the hologram. Logan and Cody were violently cheering and sweating in front of the screen. Their eyes were bloodshot, and veins rippled along their forehead and neck. They resembled beet-red gym bros who had just finished swallowing an entire bottle of steroids.

"This is amazing," Cody raved, grinding his teeth. Logan let out a loud woooo and threw his game controller against the wall. It shattered, spraying bits of plastic all over the room.

I wanna party. I wanna fight. I wanna breed. This is who I was. "This is who I am," Logan chanted incoherently while pulling off his shirt.

"Let's go!" Cody exclaimed and did a toe touch. Alan stared in horror as both men ran out of the room shirtless and in gray sweatpants.

Alan and Goddard worked tirelessly to get Cody and Logan under control and back into their bedroom. Alan wondered if he acted this crazy when on Gush and felt secondhand embarrassment for ruining his time with Luna. Goddard handed each person a beer while they started another round of virtual football.

Alan slowly sipped his while Logan and Cody guzzled theirs. Eventually, both men were intoxicated and bored with the video game.

Logan pulled up a holographic screen on his watch and started rapidly typing.

"Hey, what did she say," Cody slurred and put down his controller.

"Party at Floor 145," Logan grinned.

"Ayo," Cody cheered and gave him a high five.

"You down, lil bro?" Logan asked, pulling his shirt back on.

Alan silently nodded and made his way back to the guest room. He was relieved that his plan worked. Nerves bubbled up from his stomach to his chest. He had never been invited to one of his brother's parties. *How was he going to strike up a conversation? Let alone sell. What if he got caught?* He pulled open the dresser and grabbed the rest of the pills. He swallowed hard and prayed he had enough courage to finish the job.

All three of them changed into casual attire and made their way to the lobby of the condo complex. Alan pulled up the transportation app on his watch and typed 145 into the floating screen. He submitted the number and a pin was dropped at his location.

"Eta is in 3 mins," Alan notified them. Do you guys have everything?

Logan chugged his beer, and Cody burped in response. All three activated their space suits and waited on the docking port.

A glowing green train with a U mounted on the first cart appeared in the star-checkered sky. It curved around several flying cars and activated its bottom propulsion engines to slow down into the docking station. Alan pulled Cody and Logan back so the blue fire at the bottom of the train wouldn't damage their space suits. The doors of the train activated, and several people exited the train. They floated in and sat down at the back of the third car.

"Decompression chamber on," the PA system broadcasted, and they deactivated their space suits.

A silver robot with the number 34 etched on its chest rolled up to them.

"Can I take your order, sir?" the robot stated. Alan waved his hand while Logan and Cody ordered a round of ruby sours. They scanned their key cards using a QR code on the robot's forehead.

Thank you for your order.

The robot buzzed and pulled two red drinks from its chest. Goddard 34 wheeled away to take the next customer's order. Alan gripped the pole next to his chair as the train dove towards the lower floors. Moving downward always made him queasy. Logan and Cody pulled out their phones and began to scroll aimlessly.

Alan, enjoying the peace and quiet, watched the rise and fall of skyscrapers as they descended.

Several flying vehicles whirled around the buildings, and new hologram billboards popped up as they continued.

I don't think I have that problem, Alan thought to himself as he finished reading an advertisement for a new treatment for erectile dysfunction. The train moved towards the docking port with a big yellow sign that read Station 145 and landed.

"Floor 145," the PA system broadcasted.

Prepare for departure.

Alan activated his space suit and helped Cody and Logan leave the train. Logan scanned his key card and allowed them to enter the cube-shaped dome.

Logan banged hard on the white door while Alan and Cody waited patiently behind him. Loud music and muffled voices materialized from the door.

"Open up!" Logan exclaimed and continued to knock.

"Dude, chill out," Cody said lazily, swiping at him. Logan aggressively pushed him back. A blond woman with the number 272 embroidered in her white dress emerged from the doorway.

"Will you stop? You're going to wake my Aunt Debbie," she hissed and motioned for them to come in.

Alan was instantly overwhelmed by all the people crowded in the room. Many were casually drinking or puffing on their vapes, generating a blue haze. While several Goddards traveled around them replenishing drink orders. Alan resolved that it would be best to follow Logan and Cody. Debbie led them to the kitchen and handed them a red solo cup with dark liquid.

"What's is it?" Alan murmured.

Debbie ignored him and walked away.

Cody elbowed him in the side.

What was that?

"You are so lame, little bro," Logan commented. Everyone knows you don't talk to Debbie unless she talks to you.

"What kind of stupid rule is that?" Alan groaned.

"Hey, glasses, good to see you again," a boisterous voice boomed behind his neck. A hairy arm wrapped around Alan's neck before he could escape and put him into a chokehold. Alan's face turned bright red, and he braced himself for an uncomfortable blow to the head. He felt a bony fist collide with the top of his head and begin to drill into his skull. Alan's mind filled with distressing flashbacks of being shoved into trash cans and toilet bowls. Logan and Cody roared with laughter.

"Good to see you, Chad," Logan yelled. Alan gasped for air as the muscular arm released him and adjusted his glasses.

"No one has called me glasses since high school," Alan gasped weakly and turned around. He hated Chad's guts but knew he needed to stay. He would have to play nice.

A burly man with brown curly hair and a matching beard towered over him. Chad was now much more muscular and riddled with tattoos than in high school.

Good to see you.

"What are you up to?" Alan inquired courteously. Chad narrowed his eyes, taken aback by his friendly demeanor.

"Doing great as always," Chad boasted. I am working on my modeling career and physical physique, of course. Looks like you still need to burn off that blubber.

He poked Alan's stomach and let out an obnoxious laugh.

Alan let out a nervous laugh.

"True, true," he agreed.

Cody and Logan both exchanged baffled looks.

"Hey man, where's the real party?" Cody interrupted.

Chad grinned and led them into one of the bedrooms upstairs. Several partygoers inhaled quartz from an enormous cerulean sun in the center of the room; others were popping red bills like candy from a bowl nearby. Alan's chest tightened. This was the opportunity he was hoping for. However, he would have to use and keep his wits about him. All four joined the circle, and Alan lightly inhaled from the tube. Everyone was engaged in hushed conversation. Alan, lacking confidence in how to join, listened. He often felt like an outsider, even though others surrounded him.

A pretty brunette girl with pink butterflies in her hair and the number 894 embroidered on her dress walked in. Alan almost leaped from the floor as they locked eyes. The girl grimaced and moved to the other side of the group. She started chatting with some of the other Debbies, occasionally looking up at him in disdain. Alan stared at the floor. Just his luck, Jenny was here. He winced at the memory of him confessing his feelings and her rejection. However, Alan took a deep breath and tried to focus on the mission at hand.

He watched Chad take another red pill and wash it down with his beer.

Hey, do those hit the same as they did in high school?

No, it's like watered-down cough medicine. I'm tired of it. "I told Debbie we need something stronger, but I don't think she could get anything better from her dealer," Chad sighed.

I agree. "I personally like Gush," Alan shrugged, trying hard to appear apathetic.

Gush?

Dude, you gotta try it. "Shits, awesome," Cody interjected, taking another hit from the tube.

You got some?

Yeah.

How much?

Alan thought carefully. Hoodi told him that the pills were worth only $200, and he was going to have to split the profit with him. It might be easier to sell them

93

at a higher rate and not tell Hoodi about the extra funds.

"Only $300 each," he answered. Alan flashed him the pill bottle from his pocket. Chad raised his eyebrows and turned to Logan.

That's a bit on the cheap side. What do you think?

"I mean, I liked it," Logan shared and took a swig of his drink.

"This better not be sugar," Chad growled, activating the cash token app on his phone screen.

"Trust me, it's the real deal," Alan answered and watched as $30,000 appeared on his phone. He wanted to scream out in excitement from his sheer luck but kept his face still. Chad snatched the container from his hands and dumped the rainbow pills into the bowl.

Chapter 11

HARD TIMES

Luna and Safari ran up to the wooden bar and flagged down Beatrice. Beatrice acknowledged them and continued working on another customer's order. An old man in the center of the stage was singing an out-of-tune ballad from thirty years ago into the microphone. White light washed over him as he clung to the microphone, desperately trying to hit the song's high notes. People were engrossed in their conversations, unbothered by his lackluster performance.

"How many times is he going to sing Ole Red?" Safari groaned while rubbing her temples.

I think it's his karaoke power song. "At least he has the courage to get up there," Luna said.

She glanced back over to Beatrice. Worry was etched on her face as she rang up the following order. Luna could sense that her friend was upset about something.

"Is everything all right with Beatrice?" Luna whispered to Safari.

95

Oh, you didn't hear. "Her husband has cancer again," Safari answered, melancholy crossing over her face.

"Poor Beatrice, there has to be a way to help," Luna cried. She twirled her moon necklace in apprehension.

I think it's mainly issues with their finances. You know those treatments are expensive without insurance. Lottie told me they had been behind on their rent due to having to pay for doctor's appointments out of pocket.

"I wonder why she didn't tell me," Luna sighed. Beatrice was like a mother to her and a source of emotional support when Darnelle died. She felt conflicted. On the one hand, she wanted to be there for her friend, but she felt slightly betrayed by Beatrice telling Safari about the situation before her. Did Beatrice no longer trust her?

I think she's too proud to ask anyone for help or money. "Which we don't have anyway," Safari pointed out.

"Don't have any, what?" Beatrice announced, wearing an irritated expression.

Safari averted her gaze, but Luna looked her full in the face.

"Is it true?

What's true?

About Harold.... Tears welled up in Beatrice's emerald eyes and streamed down her round face. She quickly wiped them away, and her face became hard like a statue.

Yes, it's true. "What of it?" Beatrice said coldly. "

We want to help," Luna breathed.

Well, if you could give me $5,000 and stop gossiping about me and my family. "I would greatly appreciate it," Beatrice snapped and stormed off to the other side of the bar.

The words stung, and Luna suppressed a sob. She never enjoyed being yelled at, especially by someone she cared about. Safari patted her back in an attempt to comfort her.

I wouldn't take it personal. She's been lashing out at everyone all week. "She's just scared," Safari soothed.

"Since when did you become so wise?" Luna sniffed. I was always wise.

"You just don't listen," Safari teased.

Luna gave her a weak smile.

She and Safari discussed strategies on how to raise the $5,000. "No, that won't work. I heard that the company merged, and they aren't doing charity events anymore," Safari stated after Luna's fifth suggestion.

"Okay, well, do you have any ideas?" Luna snapped. Cause you've been shooting down all mine.

Maybe you could ask your boyfriend. "He seems like he comes from money," Safari suggested.

Who is this rich boyfriend I apparently have? "I would like to meet him," Luna said sarcastically.

Safari blinked.

Glasses…

You mean Alan?

Yeah, who else would I be talking about?

"He is not my boyfriend," Luna protested, her cheeks turned pink.

Sure…

We could never be more than friends. "It's illegal anyway, and I don't want to get beat by the authorities again," Luna said, motioning to her eye. Besides, it would be wrong to ask. I'm not just using him for money.

Safari said nothing, a smirk sprawled across her face. Luna stared back in annoyance.

"It was just a suggestion," Safari laughed. I didn't realize you would be so sensitive about it.

I'm not being sensitive. "I just think we should try something else," Luna sniffed, pulling on her necklace.

Okay. Okay, we are getting off-topic. We could easily raise the money if everyone in the ballroom donated five dollars. We could throw a party. "For charity, of course," Safari suggested.

That's actually not a bad idea. We could charge 10 dollars per person and need at least 700 people to attend. That's a typical Tuesday night when Hamburger Mary hosts bingo," Luna calculated.

"Yeah, and they pay her twenty dollars just to make the same jokes," Safari shared.

Luna almost spit out her drink.

"God, you are so evil!" Luna cried and started laughing.

"Hey, I'm just making an observation," Safari responded, flipping her braids to the side.

I like the charity idea, but planning will take some time.

"So, maybe we can host this in the ballroom at the end of the month," Luna suggested.

Would your house be able to host?

"The House of Prosperity comes to all ballroom events," Safari declared. And mother will love for all the attention to be on her. I'll also extend the invitation to the other houses.

"Maybe we can compete with them as entertainment," Luna added. It could save us a lot of money and draw the crowd we need.

I would have to ask Boris first.

But I don't foresee him saying no. "He loves Beatrice," Safari gushed.

"So, I'll be in charge of advertising and sending out invites, and maybe you can organize the event," Luna suggested, pulling up a small pocket calendar from her purse.

"Sounds good to me," Safari agreed. They continued planning the event, hopeful that they would be able to aid Beatrice.

***

Alan placed a flash drive into the bulky hard drive beside his desk. A white screen appeared on his curved desktop, and he linked his cell phone to the computer. He transferred $ 10,000 into the flash drive and then disconnected it. He labeled the flash drive *Day Pass* with a permanent marker and then put it in his dresser drawer with all his papergrams from Luna. He stared at Hoodi's contact information before pulling up the messaging app. Alan was contemplating how to address Hoodi about the pill sales. He was impressed that he could sell them in one sitting, and still had a crazy headache from that night with his brother and Cody. He was also envious of how successful Chad was. In high school, he always fantasized that he would become a successful scientist and that Chad would be working for him. However, he was still a broke loser, and Chad was thriving. *I mean, seriously, who carries around $30,000,* Alan muttered to himself.

Alan pulled open the messaging app.

Alan: They are all gone. When do you want to meet?

Hoodi: No need to meet up. We just need to wash it

Alan: Wash it? What do you mean?

Hoodi: It needs to be in ocean currency so we can invest in some of our small business owners. Do you know Harold, the owner of the Ballroom on floor five?

Alan: No.

Hoodi: You can find him by talking to his wife, the Glamour Toad.

Alan: Glamour toad? Alan was growing more confused as the conversation progressed.

Hoodi: Oh, I forgot. You're not from the Ocean Sector. I think she goes by Beatrice.

Beatrice, that name sounds familiar, Alan thought to himself.

Alan: I'll find her

Hoodi: Well, if you can't find her, ask your little girlfriend. *winky face*

Alan stared at the word girlfriend and felt a pang of unease. He secretly liked her but wasn't ready to admit it to anyone. Society reminded him that they could only be friends. Maybe Hoodi was just teasing him or trying to catch him off guard. He sent Hoodi a thumbs up and shifted his attention to getting the Day Pass.

Alan then researched the application online and then sent a blank copy to be printed out. After a few minutes, Goddard 15 intruded into the bedroom, holding a paper packet.

"Your application, sir," it buzzed and then departed. Alan's phone notifications went off from Luna. He was about to open it when Logan crashed into the room. His eyes were bloodshot, and he was grinding his teeth.

"Are you okay?" Alan asked. His brother's unkempt appearance alarmed him.

I'm fine.

I'm fine, man.

Do you, by any chance, have more Gush?

"No, sorry, I'm all out," Alan replied.

Well, can you get us some more?

No, sorry. It was a one-time thing. *Why doesn't he just do stardust like usually?* Alan thought to himself.

"I need it," Logan shouted, his fist clenching. Alan flinched. His brother would occasionally yell, but never at him. Alan did not like this new confrontational side of his brother.

"Sorry, sorry," Logan breathed and cracked his neck. I just would like to get some more. For me and my friends, of course. "Could you set me up with your plug?" Logan twitched.

"I'll talk to him first and let you know," Alan muttered.

Thanks, we appreciate it. "Just keep me updated," he declared while gesturing towards Alan.

"Yeah, man," Alan agreed, watching his brother leave the room. *That stuff is making him crazy,* Alan reflected. He turned his attention back to the application and filled out the tedious document.

He read over the document several times to check for mistakes. He asked Goddard 15 to bring him an envelope.

"Right away, sir," the robot chirped and promptly took out an envelope from the base of its chest. Alan put the application in the envelope and returned it to the robot's hands. He read that address from the website and his address to Goddard. One of the robot's hands morphed into a stamp, and it added the address.

"Send," Alan commanded.

"Yes, sir," the robot beeped and made its way to the mailroom in the condo.

"Your paper gram from Luna," the robot stated when it returned from the mailroom.

Thanks, Goddard. The robot waved goodbye as it departed. Alan admired the pink jellyfish on the brown envelope and then opened it. He read a party invitation from Luna.

Dear Alan, my friends and I are hosting a charity event for our friend Beatrice. Her husband has cancer, and we are fundraising for his treatment. Tickets are on sale for $10. Please let me know if you can come. I would love to see you there. Best wishes!

-Luna

Beatrice… no wonder that name sounded familiar, Alan thought. She was one of Luna's friends. He thought about Hoodi's instructions. So, he would have to meet her husband to wash the money. Alan didn't like where this was going. It would be easy for Luna to discover his deal with Hoodi if he talked to someone so close to Beatrice. Then again, Beatrice might work for Hoodi and not say anything. He opened the message app on his phone.

Alan: Are you going to the charity event with Beatrice?

Hoodi : Everyone is. You know now that you think of it. This might be a great way to wash the money. I want you to go and make a donation to the house that wins.

Alan: How do I know who wins?

Hoodi: They're the ones with the trophies at the end of the night.

Alan: Okay, I can do that

So, we are going to wash the money by donating it, Alan told himself. The idea felt repulsive and slimy. *I hope this is worth it,* he mumbled to himself. Alan tapped the Ocean Messenger icon on his screen. He notified Luna that he could make it to the charity event.

Chapter 12

BATTLE OF
THE HOUSES

Luna unclipped the red rope that barricaded the entrance of the ballroom. People were dressed in colorful clothing decorated with feathers and angular jewelry. The line stretched to the back of the venue, and people were still leaving elevators on different floors. Luna eagerly greeted all the guests as they flashed their invitations and handed her the entrance fee. She spotted many of her friends in the line with their respective houses. Safari's mother, Delta, led the House of Prosperity. Delta was a thin queen with long legs stretching like a spider. She was gorgeous and well-respected by the community. Yet, her remarks towards anyone were often venomous and mean-spirited, even towards her house members. She wore a long, flowing red gown with golden circles along the side and sleeves. She had red feathers protruding from the braids in her hair. Golden earrings with rubies glimmered next to her ebony face. Her house, including Safari, filled in behind her, and she wore similar dresses. They swayed extravagant, red fans with golden flowers imprinted on them.

The House of Grace pulled up behind them in demure periwinkle dresses lined with silver stars. They carried totems decorated with snowflakes and white ribbons. Delta turned behind her and made a snide remark to the queen leading the group with silver hair. The queen scowled but said nothing and fanned her pale face with a matching blue fan.

"I see Deta is up to no good," a man with a purple tuxedo commented behind Luna.

"I see nothing wrong with a little friendly competition," Luna shrugged while placing another bill in the lockbox.

Do you have everything you need to host tonight, Boris?

Boris put on sunglasses and brushed his curly hair.

"I believe so," he mused. Just let me know if you need anything. You and Safari did a wonderful job planning this, by the way. "The venue is sold out," Boris praised and pulled out a stack of cards to read over.

Thank you, anything for Beatrice. "She's the best," Luna replied.

"So, the categories are Royalty Extravaganza, Deep Ocean Realness, Ultimate Face, Life Goals, and Everlasting Diva?" Boris asked while flipping through the cards.

Yes, those seem fair. Right? "I don't want anyone to think that we are favoring the House of Prosperity, even though they are the ones hosting," Luna explained.

"I believe so, but those old queens will always have something to complain about," Boris commented.

Luna smiled and adjusted the microphone on his jacket.

"I'll see you when everyone gets in," she reassured. Boris waved and strutted into the venue. Alan appeared in front of her and held out his invitation. He looked flustered and wore a gray suit.

"Sorry for being late. I just got out of class," he mumbled while looking at the lively crowd.

"You're just in time," Luna said. I'll meet you near the bar at the portholes when everyone gets inside. Thank you for coming. It means a lot.

Alan motioned and made his way into the ballroom.

Luna turned to the next customer and was face to face with Ginger. Ginger was a Latin queen with a stocky build and lime-green eyelashes.

"Hey girl, how are you doing tonight?" Ginger roared, and the peacock feathers on her dress quivered as she spoke.

"Don't you know it's bad luck to wear Peacock feathers," Luna said, looking at her dress.

Oh, Honey, I don't need luck. "My house is going to win," Ginger announced while reapplying her lipstick.

"Oh, yes, like how my house took your trophy last week," a queen with a soft face and violet dress mouthed in front of Ginger.

"Oh my gosh, why you gotta be so negative, Sephora " Ginger boomed.

"I'm just saying," she responded in a nasally voice. "You are glowing today," Sephora motioned towards Luna's fuchsia dress.

"Thank you. I just wanted to look nice," Luna breathed, lowering her eyes.

She always hated being the center of attention.

Nice. "For someone special, I take it," Ginger insinuated.

Luna blushed. Safari really couldn't keep a secret to save her life.

"I'm sure Beatrice will think I look lovely tonight," Luna deflected.

Sure… Sephora remarked. She and Ginger looked at each other before heading in. Luna took a shaky breath and greeted the next patron.

Luna and the security guard closed the doors to the venue. She made her way around the herd of people violently shouting as the House of Royalty finished their routine. *The House of Prosperity did a wonderful job decorating,* Luna thought to herself as she looked at the new blue lanterns that hung from the ceiling. Rainbow strobe lights flashed over her as she swiftly brought the lock box to Harold's office in the back. Harold was a short man with a bald spot and black, scraggly hair around it. He was looking through his silver spectacles at a pile of yellow papers. He used to be on the heavier side like Beatrice. However, his clothes hung loosely around his body. Probably weight loss from the chemotherapy.

"Hi Harold, I think we almost hit tonight's goal," Luna proclaimed as she handed him the box.

"Thank you, this means a lot to us," Harold whispered, his eyes slightly watering. The treatments are hard on me, but it's been even harder on my B. She would never admit it, but this means the world to her. So, thank you.

"Anything to help a friend out," Luna said. I mean, you guys were there for me when Darnelle passed, so this is my way of paying you back. She peered over at the pile of yellow papers. Many of them were past due bills. She felt as if their donation didn't even make a dent in their debt. *However, something is better than nothing*, Luna said to comfort herself. She wished to be a millionaire. Money would solve all their problems.

"And now the House of Prosperity,' Boris announced from the stage.

I have to go. Safari would murder her if I missed her number. Tell Beatrice to see me when the event is over.

She hugged Harold and made her way towards the bar to find Alan.

***

Alan watched as Luna glided towards him. A dainty flower crown pulled back her soft curls, and her dress swirled around her. She looked angelic, and everything felt brighter. His heart quickened as she wrapped her arms around him, and the scent of lemons filled his nose.

"Thank you for coming," she mouthed, her brown eyes gleaming in delight, and she released him. How did the House of Prosperity do? I missed the first ten minutes of the show.

"I think they were pretty great," Alan answered hesitantly. He didn't even pay attention to the show. He spent most of the time scanning the crowd for Luna. He felt the Day Pass in his pocket. He speculated on the best time to give it to her.

Across the stage, Alan noticed a few people with black sweaters and a pink triangle at the center of their chest. He remembered the same symbol on the person who left the pills in the bathroom at the aquarium. He scanned for Hoodi. However, he was nowhere to be found. That means he couldn't see Hoodi, but Hoodi knew exactly where he was. He resolved to complete Hoodi's task first, and then give Luna the day pass.

Luna animatedly clapped as the House of Prosperity went off the stage. Another group of dancers in sapphire blue costumes and towering Victorian wigs walked onto the stage. Rhinestones were engraved in their powdered wigs and glinted under the lights.

The music echoed through the room as Boris started to excite the guests.

I present to you the House of Precious Gems.

The category is... "Royalty Extravaganza," he howled into the microphone and struck a dramatic pose with his cane that had a diamond the size of a baseball on it. The crowd screamed as the performers began to do coordinated flips and spins in heels. Alan gaped at the incredible dance. He had never experienced anything so dramatic and intense in his life. He looked over at Luna. She was filled with enthusiasm and engrossed in the performance.

The members hit their final pose at the end of the number.

The judges held their scores, and Boris broadcasted them to the crowd. 10...10...10...9....7.

The performer in the center of the stage hurled several curse words and her powdered wig at the judges. Alan was shocked when the queen was not bald. She pulled off her wig and revealed another, more petite wig.

"Get that old bag of bones off the stage," Boris jeered. The crowd roared with laughter. Some booed. The performer stormed off stage with her head held high, and the others slumped behind her.

"What was that about?" Alan inquired, amused by the dramatic scene.

"Oh, that's Queen Vanjee, she's always like that," Luna explained while twirling her flower necklace. You are unlikely to win the category when you score below an eight. I think she was mad about the seven from the last judge.

So, she threw her wig?

Luna nodded and laughed.

Two tall ladies with bright red boots and long ponytails approached them. They looked strange to Alan because they were muscular and had a prominent Adam's apple around their necks. Alan wasn't entirely sure if they were women. He had heard of men dressing up as women but had never encountered such a person. He remembered his parents referring to them as undesirables and that they could only live on lower floors. He didn't want to put his foot in his mouth, so he let Luna lead the conversation. Luna embraced the woman with tan skin and orange braids. The other one was Asian and held a tray full of red shots.

"Safari and Gina, this is my friend Alan," Luna introduced. Alan smiled and shook their hands.

"So, this is Luna's friend from the Star Sector," Gina commented, placing her hand on her hip. Her vermilion nails shimmered over her black skirt.

"Nice to finally meet you," Safari asserted, flattening her ruby dress. We've heard nothing but good things about you.

"Did you enjoy the show?" Gina asked, her dark eyes boring into him.

"Yes, I was impressed by all the jumps," Alan mumbled.

"Yeah, we got all 10s so mother won't be screaming at us tonight," Safari said.

Why would she scream?

"Our mother is very strict and demands nothing but perfection," Gina explained, pushing her sleek black hair towards her shoulder.

"Yes, she tends to throw a tantrum when we don't win, but we love her all the same," Safari continued.

"Sounds like my mother," Alan blurted out, shifting his glasses in humiliation.

Safari and Gina looked at each other and tittered.

"I guess all mothers are the same," Luna interjected and gave him a sympathetic look.

"Will we see you after the show?" Safari inquired while looking over at Alan.

"Yes, I don't see why not," Luna replied. Gina and Safari exchanged glances.

Okay, well, see you then.

"We have to deliver these refreshing beverages to our sisters," Gina groaned.

"Nice to meet you, Alan," Safari waved, and both performers departed.

"Do they dislike me?" Alan inquired. He felt like he survived an intense interrogation.

"They like you," Luna confirmed. They would insult you if they didn't. They tend to act like that when they are competing. I wouldn't take it personal. Alan directed his attention back to the stage.

After a unique array of shows and several more categories, Boris was ready to announce the winners. People ended their conversations and waited as Boris looked at his card.

And the winner is....

The House of.... Prosperity! Safari and the performers yelled in excitement and jumped up and down. Their mother stepped onto the stage and held up the gigantic aquamarine trophy. She wore a smug expression and blew kisses to the audience. The other queens glared at her in envy while the crowd rallied.

"I hope you all enjoyed the show," Boris continued. Please show your love to our amazing dancers and Beatrice by donating to Carl at the bar. The spotlight moved over to a short man with a gold chain and pink polo. He finished drying the bar and waved at the audience.

Luna was chatting about previous performances with a man wearing indigo makeup and a long feather earring. Alan placed his hand on her shoulder.

Hey, I'm going to make a donation. "I'll be right back," he informed her.

Luna acknowledged him and turned back to the man next to her. Alan made his way to Carl and waited for the mob of people around the bar to dissipate. Carl motioned for him to come up when the line cleared. He tapped on a tablet and asked Alan how much he would like to donate to the House.

"$10,000, please," Alan whispered to Carl.

Carl blinked at him.

"Like with four zeros," he confirmed slowly.

Yes.

The man said nothing and swiveled the screen towards him. "Just tap your card here," Carl instructed, motioning to the red dot on his screen. Alan opened his banking app and tapped the red dot with his phone. The red dot disappeared, and the message *Thank you for your payment* popped up on the screen. Carl thanked him, and Alan made his way back to Luna.

Alan excitedly messaged Hoodi on his phone. He notified him that the donation was delivered and that he wanted out. He felt a weight lift off his shoulders. Hoodi read the message but did not respond. Alan felt uneasy but focused on surprising Luna with the Day Pass. When he looked up from his phone, he noticed that people were staring at him and whispering to each other as he passed. He felt awkward and out of sorts. A DJ with goggles over his eyes and a top hat blasted electronic music on the stage. Luna waved to him amidst the sea of dancing people. It looked like the party wasn't going to end anytime soon. Alan wanted to find somewhere less chaotic to give Luna the Day Pass. He maneuvered around people and grabbed Luna's hand. He firmly pulled her out and to the side of the dance hall.

"Can we go somewhere quieter?" Alan asked, his voice swept up by the blaring music. Luna tapped her ear, indicating that she couldn't hear. Alan moved closer to her ear and yelled.

I can't hear.

Do you know of anywhere quieter?

Luna smiled and led him to a panel on the side of the wall. Alan was relieved to get a break from all the noise and screaming people. She pushed, and the panel swung open, leading to a translucent tunnel and ladder. Alan could see the ocean floor from the bottom of the tube, and several fish swam outside.

"If we climb up the ladder, it should take us to the alleyway that leads to the apartments close to here," Luna informed him. Many people come out here to smoke, and the area should be less crowded. Alan noticed duct tape covering certain sections of the tube.

"It's sturdy, right?" Alan inquired apprehensively. Luna followed his line of sight.

It should be safe.

"It's just old," she reassured and started climbing up the ladder. Alan followed carefully across the plastic tube.

***

Luna flung the heavy metal lid aside and climbed onto the alleyway street. She helped Alan out and secured the hatch to the ballroom transportation tube. The ground and surrounding walls were made of limestone brick. Ancient coral and fossilized shells were engraved in the aged stone. Dim lanterns hung every few feet, casting yellow light onto the alleyway. The air felt heavy and stale. A few people leaned against the wall, smoking near the entrance. Luna held Alan's hand and led him down the dark corridor. As they descended, the walls curved and shifted. She felt Alan's hand grow sweaty and realized the alleyway probably felt alien and confining for him. Luna wanted Alan to be comfortable. So, she settled on bringing him to the Angelfish Courtyard. It was a bit more spacious and pumped fresh air from floor eight.

Luna located a stone archway with a triangular fish painted on the top and stopped. She led Alan into the courtyard. A lapis pool was in the center of the room, and zebra-patterned fish swam around it. The wall displayed a mosaic of a triangular fish with wispy fins, and a stone bench was placed underneath it. Fresh, cool air rippled through a metal grate placed above the ceiling. Luna brushed cigarette buts off the stone slab and sat down. Alan joined her, studying the graffiti sprayed on the walls.

"Quiet enough for you?" Luna asked, pulling her knees towards her chest.

"Yes, much better," Alan sighed.

You know, this was my favorite place as a kid. I used to feed the fish bread until I learned it upsets their stomach. I see why you like it.

"It's like a mysterious stone cave," Alan whispered and touched the tiny squares of the mosaic.

A toilet flushed above, interrupting them.

I guess we aren't in a cave then.

I wish. We are actually underneath a casino on floor six. "Everything is built on top of each other down here," Luna explained.

Luna rested her head on her knees and looked up at Alan. His eyes were like pools of honey behind his glasses. Everything felt distant and slow. She felt like she was drowning. She realized she was gawking at him and pulled herself out of the surreal moment. She sat up. Butterflies fluttered in her stomach. *Nope, nope. Let's not think about that,* she told herself. She blinked a few times and placed her hands on the stone bench to steady herself.

So, uh. So, what did you need to ask me?

Alan pulled out a white card and handed it to her.

The words *Day Pass* and a black star shimmered on the front of the card. Luna looked at Alan and then back to the card in disbelief. In all her life, she would never have believed that she would hold one of these cards. She couldn't access the Land Sector, let alone the Star Sector.

"Is this for me?" she gasped, her hands shaking.

Yes. Her chest filled with gratitude.

"It must have been extremely hard to get this," Luna croaked.

Why? Why me? Alan said nothing, but his eyes were full of emotion. Luna could only hear her heartbeat as they sat in silence.

Because..." I like you," he murmured. And I want you to be with me without getting arrested or beaten up. He hesitated.

Do you like me?

Luna couldn't speak or bring herself to admit how she felt. Instead, she leaned closer to his face and placed her palms on his chest. She knew this was a bad idea. She could hear her mother and Beatrice screaming at her in the back of her head. Her heart did not care. Alan's eyes widened, and his breath quickened, but he didn't move. Luna tilted her head and kissed him. His lips were warm, but they trembled as they kissed. Luna immediately pulled away and placed her hand over her mouth. *That was a terrible idea,* she scolded herself, looking towards the blue pond. Panic washed over her.

Alan wrapped his arms around her back and pulled her towards him. He tenderly placed his hand on her neck and kissed her back deeply. Luna closed her eyes in acceptance. Her body was set ablaze. Luna felt his hand brush up her skirt and against her thighs. She immediately pulled back and held his hands.

"Sorry," he flushed and pulled away.

It's okay, just not here. "It's not very private," she murmured, glancing towards the archway. She picked up the pass from the ground and held it.

"So, when can I visit?" she inquired, trying to catch her breath.

"I was thinking tomorrow or as soon as you can," Alan said, stroking her back. It expires in thirty days.

I'll be there. Luna embraced him.

Thank you. There's no way I could ever pay you back.

"So, thank you," Luna whispered in his ear.

Alan drew closer, but Luna heard footsteps echo down the alleyway. She pulled away and put the Day Pass in her purse. She quickly fixed her hair and flatted her dress. Disappointment flooded Alan's face, and he sat up. Beatrice walked in with a lit cigarette on her red lips and shot daggers at Alan.

What are y'all doing down here? "We were looking all over for you," Beatrice scowled, displeased with the scene before her.

"Just getting some fresh air," Luna replied, flashing a smile. Alan was slightly overwhelmed by the commotion, so I was just showing him somewhere quieter.

Mmm hmm, Beatrice responded in disbelief.

"Well, curfew is about to start, so you should probably get home," Beatrice told Alan. Luna could sense that she was restraining her anger.

Luna and Alan followed Beatrice back to the Ballroom. The lights were on, and many guests were loading into the elevators.

"Luna has to help clean up," Beatrice informed Alan. Thank you for coming, and have a great night.

"Take care," Alan waved and made his way home.

"Come on," Beatrice commanded, and Luna followed her to the back office. Luna stood in front of the desk, anticipating Beatrice would start yelling at her. It never came. Instead, Beatrice plopped down before the yellow papers and rubbed her eyes. She breathed in and looked up at Luna. Her face was severe.

What are you doing?" she asked in a low voice.

"Just talking," Luna lied.

"I think you were doing more than just talking," she responded, fury cracking in her voice. You know it's illegal for you to be with him. "You know they will kill you when they find out," Beatrice said, her words cutting like knives in Luna's chest.

"Yes," Luna swallowed.

Okay, then I'll ask the question again. What are you doing with him?

It's not like that," Luna protested, holding her arm behind her back.

Then, please explain what it's like, because I've been hearing things. And I usually don't pay attention to rumors, but I just caught you two alone together. So, that's why I'm asking.

Luna knew she wouldn't win the argument, so she said nothing.

Look, I know it seems like I'm being mean, but I've seen this before. You think you can hide your relationship, and they won't find out. But the authorities always do. And they won't punish him, but they will punish you.

Luna swallowed hard and knew Beatrice was right. She had heard this from her mom her entire life. The phrases *Don't talk to them. Don't associate. Keep your head down,* reverberated in the back of her head.

Luna felt torn and lost. She knew Beatrice was trying to keep her safe, but the opportunity to be in the Start Sector and see Alan was too tempting.

"You're right, I'm sorry," Luna trembled. "I won't see him again," she lied. Beatrice sighed and hugged her. Luna buried her face in her shoulder. She wanted to cry, to scream, but kept her emotions still.

"I just want you to be alive and safe," Beatrice murmured in her ear.

Are you gonna tell my mum? Luna asked nervously. She imagined her mom howling with rage and throwing items around the room. Beatrice paused for a moment.

"No," she decided. You're grown. You can make your own decisions.

Safari and Delta chatted jovially as they entered the room. They sensed the tension between them and stopped. Delta broke the uncomfortable silence.

"Thank you, Beatrice, for allowing the House of Prosperity to host today," she said, holding up the trophy. Of course.

"I think it's time for all of us to retire," Beatrice remarked.

Luna waved goodbye and followed Safari and Delta out of the office. Relief washed over her as she escaped Beatrice's intense probing.

"What happened?" Safari mouthed behind Delta. Luna signaled that she would tell her later. At the moment, she was torn between her safety and what her heart wanted.

Chapter 13

DAY PASS

"You did what!" Safari exclaimed, jumping off the bed. Luna shushed her.

Will you be quiet? "No one can know," Luna uttered while brushing her hair. Safari held her hands over her mouth in shock and stood silently for a moment.

"Girl, you could have died," Safari screeched, slapping her knees.

I wouldn't have. He admitted his feelings first. "That's why I need you to stop telling all my business to your house," Luna snapped, putting her hairbrush down.

With all due respect, I didn't say anything. You're the one who keeps smiling at him, hugging him, and bringing him to all our events. People are not stupid. "They are going to put two and two together," Safari retorted.

Luna sighed and started applying her makeup. "Did I really make it that obvious?" she moaned, dipping her brush into the pink eye shadow.

"Yes, but you were in deep denial," Safari confirmed.

Trust me, I know I'm not supposed to like him, but I do. He's really sweet, and he listens to me when I talk about my interests. "Most people tune me out when I start talking about science," Luna explained, lightly applying the brush to her eye. He also gave me a Day Pass. It's literally worth my entire year's salary at the plant, and I didn't ask for it. So, I can't just not go.

"So, you really about to put your life in danger over some dick," Safari expressed, crossing her arms.

"Really!" Luna huffed and glared at her.

It's not like that.

Well, I'm just trying to keep it real. "I don't think it's a good idea, and you're just being hard-headed about it," Safari protested.

I know, but this might be the only chance I get up there, and he worked so hard to get it for me. "I have to go," Luna asserted, putting on her lipstick. Safari walked over to her jewelry box and pulled out a necklace with miniature roses on it.

"Here, wear this," Safari ordered, placing it around Luna's neck. It will compliment your makeup. They both stared into the mirror.

"I'm scared," Luna admitted, studying her reflection.

"I know," Safari replied. But you've made up your mind, and I'll be here when you get back. Luna smoothed down the lace on her sleeves and sprayed strawberry perfume on her neck.

How do I look?

"Lovely as always," Safari responded and sat back on the bed. Luna pulled out her white sandals and black heels and analyzed them.

"So, will you let him get to the next base?" Safari inquired with a sly expression. You could join the mile-high club.

"I'm too scared," Luna confessed, tying the sandals. I've never been with a guy before.

It's not complicated. "You just-" Safari started.

"Don't worry, I know how it works. It just seems scary and kinda embarrassing," Luna interrupted. You know, at my age.

"Well, guys like that," Safari commented. Just try to relax.

Safari, nothing is going to happen. "I'm just visiting," Luna interjected.

Well, you said you were just friends, and now you're kissing. I'm just looking out for you.

Luna shot her an annoyed look but smiled. She knew that her friend was trying to help. "Alright, wish me luck," Luna sighed and made her way out.

Luna pulled out the pass and scanned it. As she ascended to the higher floors, she grew more and more excited. She pulled out the paper Alan had sent her and tried memorizing the instructions. *So, I have to get clearance on Floor 150, and then Alan will meet me at the courtyard near entrance A,* Luna confirmed, placing it into her purse.

The elevator stopped at Floor 150, and Luna walked into a blank, white room with hundreds of people standing in line. Many were in business attire, talking on a phone or tapping on a transparent screen from their wrist. They were steadily shuffling through several rows of rope towards a worker dressed in a white uniform and wearing gloves. The worker would grab their key cards, scan them, and type information into a computer. Silver robots with mechanical wings floated above the people. They carried packages into several doors in the wall that would automatically open and close. Everyone in the room looked miserable. Luna was taken aback by the chaos but thankful she arrived early.

An orange robot holding a clipboard rolled up to her. It had four optic eyes and the number 978 etched on its chest. This must be the Goddard that Alan explained in his letter. *He might be able to help me,* Luna reflected, relief washing over her.

"Hi Goddard 978, can you please help me get to the day pass checkpoint," Luna said to the robot and held out the Day Pass. The robot tilted its head and buffered for a moment.

"Certainly," it beeped. Just scan the Day Pass and your key card to log in.

Luna analyzed the robot and didn't see a keypad anywhere on its body.

"You have to tap the QR code on the top of its head," a voice instructed behind her.

Luna turned around. An irritated woman carrying a briefcase stood behind her. She had short red hair and wore a name tag that said 457.

"Oh, thank you," Luna said, stepping to the side to get out of her way. The woman paused and looked at her pink blouse.

Where's your name tag?

"Oh, I haven't gotten mine yet," Luna admitted. I think I still need to get registered.

Are you from the Land Sector?

"Yeah," Luna lied.

The woman sneered and moved towards the long line. *It's good I didn't tell her where I lived. She might have called the authorities,* Luna thought to herself. She noticed the QR code on the robot's head and scanned both cards.

"Thank you," the robot buzzed. Please follow me.

Goddard 978 led her past all the business people standing in line. Many of them paused and gaped at her as she passed. *Maybe my flamingo pink dress wasn't the way to go. I should have worn something more modest,* she scolded herself. She heard a scratching sound behind her. Luna turned in horror and noticed she was leaving muddy footprints on the tile floor. The scratching sound was from a miniature robot scrubbing the floor clean. Luna quickened her pace. She was only in a new sector for five minutes and was already causing a spectacle. She desperately wanted to become invisible.

Goddard stopped before an ivory welcome desk with two people typing into computers. One was a clean-shaven man with a name tag labeled Greg, and the other was a woman with a name tag that read 254. Goddard and the miniature robot bowed and departed into the wall. The man looked up from his computer.

"What can I do for you?" he sniffed.

"I'm here to use my Day Pass," Luna replied, handing him the white card. The man sneered at her outstretched hand and pulled a bottle of Germ X from his pocket. He squeezed some clear liquid onto his palm and rubbed his hands together. He took the key card and scanned it. Luna was unnerved by his rudeness. She wasn't dirty.

Can I have your Sector card? Luna handed him the blue key card. He looked at the symbol on the card and narrowed his eyes. Luna was growing concerned that they weren't going to let her in. The man finished typing into the computer and gave her back the key card.

The woman glanced up from her computer screen.

"You aren't going in like that," she gasped.

" I don't have anything else to wear," Luna defended.

"She has a Day Pass," Greg informed his coworker. I'm printing the badge right now. He got up and walked into a door labeled Authorized Personnel. The woman nodded.

"So, you are going to go in the door label Operations over to the right here to go through check-in procedures," the woman instructed, pointing to the right wall.

You must take a health exam, disinfection procedure, and wear our uniforms. If you need help, you can ask any of your stupid questions to Goddard 900 by using the Day Pass. Please return your uniform, badge, and hologram watch at 10 am tomorrow at the welcome desk. If you do not check out on time, you will be escorted out and have a 30-day ban. The woman pulled out a clipboard with several lines highlighted.

"Please sign her, here, and here," she motioned.

Luna grabbed one of the office pens and added her signature. The lady pulled out an ink pad.

"Dip your thumb into the inkpad and put it on the bottom of the contract in the box right there," she directed. Luna followed the instructions and stamped her thumbprint on the document.

Goddard!

"Wipes," she screeched at the wall.

A robot holding a warm towel appeared from the wall. Luna whipped her hands clean with the towel, and the robot handed her a dry towel from the center of his chest. Luna handed it back, and it swerved away.

Greg walked back into the room, holding a watch and name tag. Please put these on after you finish the check-in procedures. He handed them to Luna, and she thanked them. The desk attendants didn't respond and resumed typing on their monitors. She entered the Operations door. The room had a bed and a tubular machine around it. Goddard 978 rolled up to her.

"Please lay on the bed for the health exam," it beeped. Luna got on the bed and faced the machine. Goddard pulled up next to her, and a hologram screen was broadcasted from two lenses on the top of his head. He started interacting with the translucent hologram.

"Starting health exam," he announced. Red lights appeared from the top of the tube, and it scanned her body. It started to spin and readjust. Then, the tube moved from her feet to her head and back down. The machine shut off. The robot displayed a computer model of her body. You have two tumors. One on your right lung and the other in your stomach. Would you like to remove them?

Luna gawked at the two dark spots on the screen. She was only in her 20s. How could she already have cancer?

"Will it hurt?" she questioned the robot.

"Our state-of-the-art technology in the Star Sector makes treatment painless," it buzzed.

" I don't want the cancer to stay in my body," Luna reasoned. She thought of her grandmother in a hospital bed with hair falling out and Harold.

"Yes, I want to try," she told the robot.

131

"Please lie back on the bed," it instructed. This time, a blue light scanned Luna's body, followed by a red light again.

"Cancer has been removed," Goddard buzzed and displayed an image without the black spots. Luna thought of Harold and was disheartened. Here, she was able to cure cancer in a matter of seconds, and he had to pay thousands of dollars to pump poison into his body. She knew her friend would be angry with her for breaking her promise, but Beatrice had to know about this new cancer treatment.

Hey Goddard, do they have this machine in all Sectors or just the Star Sector?

"Health Treatment 3003 is found in the Star and Cloud Sectors," the robot responded. Luna perked up. Maybe Beatrice and Harold can get their treatments in the Cloud Sector. She would have to ask Alan how he got a Day Pass.

"Shall we continue?" the robot beeped.

"Yes," Luna replied and dismounted the bed. The next room opened to a spa with a pink and gold color scheme. The welcome desk had two magenta robots floating behind it. They had the number 12 painted on them, and their bodies were more feminized compared to the previous goddards she met. The orange goddard rolled back into the last room.

"Welcome," the female robots beeped. Are you ready for disinfection?

Yes, please. Luna followed the robot to a pool with lots of bubbles. Various luxurious beauty products were organized on shelves, and the smell of vanilla wafted in the air. On the other side of the room were mirrors and hairstyle chairs next to them.

"Please place your clothes on the chair and go into the bath," the robot instructed.

Luna timidly took off her clothes and covered her body. She slid into the bath, and her muscles immediately relaxed as the warm water, herbs, and salts caressed her body. She felt like a mermaid and swam around in the bubbles.

"We need to wash your hair," the robot buzzed. It carried a clay pot over her head, and warm water was poured with rose petals mixed in. The robot began washing her hair and combing tangles out of it.

"What scent would you like for your bath?" the other robot beeped.

"Do you have strawberry?" Luna grinned. Most certainly. The robot handed her a white bottle and luffa. Luna scrubbed her body, enjoying the fruity aroma, and placed the items on the edge of the bath.

"Are you ready to dry?" both robots chimed.

Luna grabbed the towels that the robots were holding. She wrapped her hair in one and dried her body with the other. The first robot pulled a tape measure and started measuring parts of her body. The other held up a tablet with different clothing options.

Click on the item you would like to wear today. All the options were lovely but in white. She opted for the lacey dress with long sleeves and tapped the submit button. Another robot rushed in, carrying the dress in its arms. Luna dressed and felt weird with all the robots serving her. The robots led her to the chairs in front of the mirrors. One removed a blow dryer and straightened iron from a storage compartment in its tubular body. The others morphed their hands into metal cups.

"Please stick your hands and feet in for your manicure and pedicure," the robot said as it held up its cup-shaped hands. Luna didn't want to, but the robots continued hovering in place. She carefully placed her hands and feet into the cups. She felt the tips of her fingers and toes being scrubbed and dried. The cups made strange whirling and grinding sounds.

She prayed she wouldn't lose a toe or finger today. The robots pulled away and held out a lotion bottle. Her finger and nails were now painted white and sparkling. Luna added some lotion to her palm and rubbed her hands together. While this was happening, the other robot pulled out three arms. One arm blow-dried her hair. The other combed it, and the last one flattened it with an iron.

After five minutes, her curls were straightened into the silky-smooth hair that hung down her back. Luna admired her transformation in the mirror. She had no idea her hair was this long. Another robot brought her a tray with various golden jewelry and stylized white headbands. She used the headband with daisies to push back her hair and added thin gold bracelets onto her wrist. She put Safari's rose necklace back on. She thought it would bring her luck.

She stared at her face in the mirror; it looked plain, without makeup.

Do you have any makeup? The robots all beeped and descended into a shaft in the wall. They came back with two trays. One had lotions, and the other just had mascara and pink lipstick.

"This is the only makeup approved for visitors," it buzzed. Luna was slightly disappointed. In the Ocean Sector, everyone wore dramatic and colorful makeup. However, something was better than nothing. She moisturized her face and reapplied her makeup. She studied her reflection. It was like staring back at a stranger. Would Alan even recognize her?

Luna gave the robots her old clothes, and they confirmed they would be waiting for her at the welcome desk. Luna fastened the pearl white space boots. She put on her name tag, DP 12678, and the watch. The watch didn't show the time but was a blank glowing screen.

"How do you work this?" she asked the goddard closest to her. The robot instructed her to tap on the screen, and when she completed the task, the hologram popped up. The robot showed her the basic mechanics of the watch. Luna was astounded by the convenience of it. She could make a phone call, get directions, order food, watch a movie, or do various other things at her fingertips. She realized Alan must've been frustrated when he visited her. The

Ocean Sector hardly had elevators that would work. She wondered how she could even describe this world to her friends. It was so contrary to her own.

The robot handed her a small white purse where she could carry her card and directed her out of the building. She stepped onto a magnificent courtyard that was enclosed in a glass dome. On the inside of the dome, a hologram screen of clouds floated past a sun in the middle. Animated bluebirds would occasionally fly past the yellow ball of fire. Around the hologram, you can see the void of space with billions of stars in the distance. Palm trees were planted around the courtyard with a variety of tropical flowers. A white sidewalk with benches led to a marble statue of an astronaut at the center of the courtyard. It had the words Star Capital engraved at the base of it. Luna felt as if she entered paradise. Everything was fresh, clean, and opulent.

Luna sat down on one of the golden benches. She tapped her watch and activated the screen. She moved through the different apps and found a map of her location. She confirmed that she was in Courtyard A, as Alan instructed her. She pushed through some of the other apps and found a message board. She could message him and let him know she was here. She tapped the icon and pulled out the instructions Alan sent her. She saw the number 00125678 in the left-hand corner. She typed the number into the contact bar of the message board. Alan's face appeared on her screen, and the name Alan Smith was displayed on the bottom. *So, that's his last name,* she thought and began typing her message. She hit submit and waited for a response. Three dots formed in the chat bubble.

Alan: "Where are you?"

Luna: Next to the astronaut statue

Alan: I'll find you

This was way faster than sending paper grams.

Luna closed the screen and took in the picturesque scene. Not many people were in the courtyard, but a few were talking on the phone or at a hologram screen. They seemed absorbed in screens, missing out on the splendor of their surroundings. Luna felt blessed to be here, but it was nothing like she had heard or imagined. She thought people would be jubilant and flaunt giant stacks of money covered in jewels. However, everyone she saw wore gray and was constantly distracted. She thought about Alan and where he would take them. Would they have to act differently while they were here? Luna watched as cameras above the building's exit zoomed in on her. She was positive she was being monitored and recorded. She thought about what Beatrice said to her the night before. She needed to be careful.

***

Alan read the message on his phone. She was here. He was still conflicted about the events that unfolded the night before. He anticipated a pat on the back or awkward silence. That's how most of his interactions went with women. Instead, he was given his first kiss.

However, he felt unhappy that he couldn't tell anyone for fear of getting in trouble. His mind drifted to her soft lips and running his hands up her skirt. He shook his head at the dirty thoughts and ran his fingers through his brown hair. Alan knew he had to be on his best behavior. He didn't want to draw any more unwanted attention. They were already on thin ice. Alan mounted a hoverboard on the docking station. The engines started, and it propelled him into space.

Alan arrived at the courtyard and hopped off the hoverboard. He attached it to the public charging port and entered the bubble dome. Walking past the tropical foliage, he noticed a beautiful woman with glossy black hair gingerly touching flowers on a vine. Her hair shimmered in the fluorescent light, and warmth spread across his cheeks. The woman turned around, and Alan recognized Luna. Her face was glowing and full of exhilaration.

"Why are you standing in the bushes?" Alan laughed and approached her.

I got bored and saw this bush had lots of butterflies on it.

"Look," she squeaked and pointed to a blue butterfly on one of the white flowers.

Yeah, they are lovely. Alan noticed that several people were looking in their direction. They were drawing attention.

"Are you ready to go?" he asked. Luna nodded and hopped back onto the sidewalk.

How did check-in go? "No issues, I hope," Alan said as they made their way to the docking port.

I think it went well. "I don't think they liked me very much," Luna answered, explaining her experience with the welcome desk attendants.

Oh, I know Greg from high school, and he was like that towards everyone. "He sucked," Alan said.

Oh good, that makes me feel better.

So, where are we going?

"It's a surprise," Alan answered. Do you know how to use your hologram watch?

Sort of.

"The robots showed me some of the basic things, but I'm not exactly an expert," Luna admitted.

Here, let me help you. Alan tapped on her watch and demonstrated how to activate the space suit. Luna shrieked as the suit jumped out of the watch and covered her body.

You can help me take this off, right?

"Yes," Alan reassured and deactivated the suit.

"That was not what I was expecting," Luna admitted, putting her space suit back on.

They arrived at a metal door that led to the outside of the enclosure.

Ready?

Luna nodded. Alan led her to the docking station and put in their coordinates for the metro. Luna stood frozen in place and started hyperventilating. Alan followed her line of sight. She was staring down the edge of the docking port into space.

"We are really high up," she trembled. Alan stood in front of her to block her view.

Just take a few deep breaths. "We are safe," he said calmly, rubbing her arms.

Are you scared of heights?

"A little," Luna replied, her breath slowed.

It's completely safe. If you were to fall off, your space suit would activate and pull you back onto the docking port. Luna looked unconvinced.

Here, you can hold my hand if it makes you feel safer.

Luna grabbed onto it like it was a life raft.

Thanks. "Sorry, I kinda freaked out," Luna whispered. A train with a yellow M mounted on the first car snaked around the skyscrapers on the higher floors and dove down to the docking port.

I don't... "I don't think I can do this," Luna pleaded, her face contorted in fear.

I know you can. The train will only go up if it makes you feel any better. We can use the elevators to head back down. It'll be okay," Alan consoled.

Luna breathed in and nodded. Alan helped Luna climb into the car and led her to a seat in the back. The vehicle was highly full due to many people heading home from work. Alan helped Luna deactivate her space suit. She shoved her face into his shoulder as they launched upward.

Alan wrapped his arm around her and continued to hold her hand. "You're missing the view," he murmured in her ear.

Luna looked up at him.

"You're sure we won't fall," she whispered.

Alan nodded his head. She looked out the window, and her face was filled with bliss. Alan's gaze drifted from her neck to the roses that danced around her cleavage. He realized that he was ogling her and averted his gaze.

"You're so brave," she said to him. If you weren't here, I would have run back home. Her face grew closer to his, and Alan felt tempted to kiss her again. He could feel eyes on his back and lifted his arm. Luna shifted away and looked back out the window.

Alan and Luna left the Metro and entered an octagonal dome with the number 157 posted on top of it. They approached a warehouse with a sign that displayed Star-Mart in glowing red and blue letters. Several goddards were pushing shopping carts into the store, and flying cars lined up at the front to drop off customers. A hologram of a fashion model appeared above the store. She held up a white tube of toothpaste and flashed her perfect teeth.

We are going to pick up some dinner for this evening. "Just let me know what you want to eat," Alan explained.

Luna was dumbfounded by the variety of goods in the supermarket. Anything and everything was in the store. Luna was tempted to pick fish, which the main

141

thing she ate at home. However, she wanted to try something new. Every few feet, a hologram or screen showcasing an advertisement would appear. At first, Luna was intrigued but grew annoyed as they constantly popped up.

"What do you usually eat?" Luna asked. I don't recognize anything here.

"We could get some chicken salad sandwiches," Alan suggested. My mom would get them in bulk when we camped as kids in the Land Sector.

Have you tried them?

No.

Are you okay with mayonnaise?

"I've never tried chicken," Luna confessed.

What?!

"Most people eat fish on my floor," Luna explained. It's usually costly to get other meats because of the tariffs from the Land Sector.

"That must get old after a while," Alan stated.

It's not so bad if you season it right.

"Well, we have to try some chicken while you're here," he said, adding the sandwiches to the cart.

"What are these?" Luna inquired, holding up a green and white striped fruit.

Those are watermelons from the Cloud Sector.

That's so cool! "I've only eaten it from a can," Luna exclaimed. Alan recoiled at the thought of canned watermelon.

Then, we have to add it to the cart. He placed the mini watermelon next to the sandwiches.

Would you like anything for dessert?

I usually have a nightcap. "The dentist says I need to take it easy on the sweets," Luna joked.

Alan led her to the beverage aisle and let her pick out a bottle of wine. He had a goddard bring them a few other items to complement the dinner.

"Looks good," Luna said, peering into the cart.

A green goddard with the Star-Mart logo wheeled up to them. He scanned the cart with lasers from his eyes.

"$46.95," it beeped, placing the items in a picnic basket. Alan tapped his key card on its head and carried the basket out of the store. I feel like I've seen more robots than people today.

"Where is everyone?" Luna asked. Most people are working in offices or remotely.

"The goddards mainly work the services jobs here," Alan answered.

So, I guess most people are white-collar, like lawyers and businessmen.

Yes.

Is that why you have to be an accountant? The sincerity of the question caught Alan off guard. He hesitated.

"Yes," he replied and grimaced.

It's just part of life.

Luna gave him a sympathetic look.

I know how that feels. "I sometimes feel like I'm going to die at that Tilapia plant," Luna shared.

Chapter 14

THE OBSERVATORY

Alan and Luna approached a massive rotunda with a telescope pointing out from the top. Several satellite dishes on columns positioned around the building rotated towards the sky. The hologram screen at the top of the glass dome dissipated from the daytime display to the night sky.

"What happened to the sun?" Luna inquired and pointed at the dome ceiling.

"It's switching from day mode to night time," Alan responded. It's probably around 6.

Oh, okay.

"So, you still haven't told me where we are going." she continued.

This is the Solar Observatory, which is the best place for stargazing. Luna gasped in excitement.

"I thought you might like it," Alan grinned.

Luna was greeted by a colossal telescope planted at the heart of a freshly cut lawn and a coliseum of benches surrounding it. The observatory reminded Luna of a sports stadium.

Do you want to sit out on the lawn or on the benches?

Which has the better view?

I like the lawn. "You get to lie down," Alan said.

Makes stargazing comfortable.

Well, I don't want to be uncomfortable," Luna said.

"Lawn it is," he mumbled and scanned the key card.

A goddard carrying a picnic blanket followed them and placed it in front of the telescope. Alan dropped the basket and motioned for Luna to sit with him.

Luna sat down and adjusted her skirt. Alan handed her both glasses and poured wine into them. Luna thanked him and handed him back one of the glasses.

"Cheers," Luna sounded, and they tapped the glasses. Luna savored some of the wine. It tasted sweet and made her face feel warm. She finished it in one gulp.

"Can I have another one?" she hiccupped, holding her glass. Alan glanced at the empty glass, slightly alarmed.

"Make sure you save this for dinner," he said, refilling the class.

I will. "Sorry," Luna blushed and held the glass on her lap. She scanned the benches and her surroundings. A few people were here and there, but it was, for the most part, empty.

"Where is everyone?" she asked.

"Most people don't come to the observatory on a Friday night," Alan answered, crossing his legs. Most people are out partying.

Well, I guess we aren't like most people. "We're better," Luna grinned and flipped her hair.

"I agree," Alan laughed and put the wine back in the basket.

A goddard handed Luna and Alan a pamphlet on constellations they would see tonight. Luna placed it into her purse while Alan read his. She was ecstatic to show Safari later.

"Are you hungry?" Alan asked and pulled more items out of the basket. Luna nodded. Alan handed her one of the chicken sandwiches. Luna bit into it and savored the delicious meal. The meat was much earthier and less salty than the fish Luna was used to eating, but she appreciated her meal.

Alan held the watermelon and pulled out a small gray tube. He pushed a button on the side. A mini green laser appeared from the top of the tube, and he sliced the watermelon into fours.

"Did you just cut that with a laser?" Luna gasped in disbelief.

Yeah.

"I'm not allowed to bring knives into public places like this," Alan confirmed, putting the laser back into his pocket.

That's so cool.

Luna bit into the watermelon. It was sweet and crunchy. It was a thousand times better than the canned watermelon she ate as a kid, which was dry and tasteless.

You're all quiet. "I take it's good," Alan shared before biting into his sandwich.

Luna beamed and devoured her watermelon.

The lights dimmed, and luminous stars appeared on the ceiling. Luna was captivated by the galaxies and planets that rolled across the ceiling. The visuals were detailed and hypnotic. Luna wrapped her arms around her knees, enchanted by the space theme show. Luna felt Alan's arm wrap around her. She tore her gaze away from the heavens and looked up at him. He didn't move and continued looking up at the screen. She then looked back at the stands. The observatory was deserted, and a few looked up at the light show. Luna gently rested her head on his shoulder. She knew it might bring attention to them but couldn't pull away. She heard his heart beating rapidly.

"He's probably just as nervous as I am," she thought. Luna stayed in place and held his hand. She kept her eyes on the blur of constellations, relishing this perfect moment.

***

"So, what did you think of the show? "Alan asked as they left the observatory. It was amazing.

"I loved it so much," Luna raved. Alan was ecstatic that everything went well during their time together. He found Luna to be sweet and felt like he could be himself around her.

So, uhh. "Are we going to do anything else tonight?" she asked, clasping her hands behind her back and swaying with anticipation. Alan paused, and a wicked idea crept into his mind. He knew he shouldn't ask, but he would regret it if he didn't try. He shoved his hands into his pockets.

If you want, we could get a nightcap at the apartment. Alan instantaneously regretted the question as soon as it left his lips. He probably startled her by being too forward.

Luna hesitated and then blushed.

Okay… "I'd love to," she breathed timidly. It's just a nightcap, right?

Yeah, if that's what you want," he answered, his stomach dropping in disappointment. No pressure.

Luna gave him a shy smile and pulled on her rose necklace. Thoughts were racing through Alan's head as they entered the elevator. He was shocked that she agreed and was brainstorming ideas to impress her.

Alan closed the door to his parents' condo and was relieved that no one was home.

"Hey goddard, where is everyone?" he announced. A robot appeared.

"Your parents have departed on a flight to Boda Boda in the Cloud Sector Resorts, and Logan's location is turned off," goddard buzzed.

Thank you, Goddard.

The robot bowed and moved into the next room.

It would have been nice if they told me they were going on vacation, Alan thought. *And Logan was probably somewhere he shouldn't be.*

"Is this your house?" Luna asked, interrupting his thoughts.

No, it's my parents. I plan on moving out when I finish school.

"They have interesting taste," Luna said, pointing at the infamous semicolon sculpture. The sculpture was a hideous piece of artwork that was made of human pubic hair. Alan and his brother hated it, but his mother insisted they showcase it in the living room.

"Is that hair?" she asked tentatively while looking at the artwork closer.

Yes.

"Whenever I look at it, I want to burn it," he remarked, expressing his disdain.

"Sounds like you have better taste," Luna said. Why did they buy it?

"My mom is obsessed with what's trending, and this is the latest trend," Alan explained in an exacerbated tone.

"Sounds exhausting," Luna sympathized.

You have no idea.

"The apartment is still beautiful," Luna continued.

"So, I know the artwork is interesting, but I think you'll like the view better," Alan proclaimed and motioned towards the patio. Luna waited outside on the patio bench while Alan summoned Goddard in the kitchen.

"Goddard, what drink would be best for the end of the night?" he asked the robot. He was unsure of what Luna would want. Goddard's chest plate transformed into a screen.

"These are popular beverages in the Ocean Sector," it beeped. Alan touched the screen and surveyed the options. He selected an Irish coffee, and Goddard pulled out the beverages from his chest cavity.

"Two Irish coffees, sir," it buzzed. Alan thanked the robot and made his way to the patio.

He handed Luna the coffee, and they sat silently, admiring the city lights.

"Alan…" she whispered, breaking the silence. Why do you like me?

Alan couldn't express his feelings, so he made an awkward, breathy shushing sound. Luna looked over, amused.

"I didn't quite catch that," she smiled. Why don't you tell me? "I mean, you're the one who kissed me first," Alan blurted out. He flinched at his tone-deaf outburst and faced the overlook. *God, I am so lame*, he thought, warmth spreading over his cheeks. Luna giggled.

Okay….

You're kind and intelligent. And handsome…

"And quite the gentleman," she said, tenderly holding his hand. Alan's chest swelled from the praise, and his palms tingled from her touch.

"It's just too bad society doesn't approve of us," her voice cracked with sorrow. She slid closer to Alan and rested her head on his shoulder. Alan's heart leaped, but he couldn't look at her.

"Alan, you're a great person," she continued. And if we could be together, I'd be lucky to have you. I just want you to know that.

Alan was lost for words and was overtaken with endearment. He never had anyone care for him like this. He didn't want to let her go. Alan set his drink down and turned to her.

"What if we could be?" he asked, leaning towards her face.

Luna shook her head. I can't ask that of you. I can't alienate you from your family and friends. From the people in your life. Her eyes watered.

It hardly matters. They don't talk to me anyway. They think I'm weird that I'm a loser. "You don't make me feel like that," Alan confessed, pulling her closer.

Luna gazed intently at him.

I can't…"They'll arrest me, you know," she murmured.

They won't find out.

"You don't know that," Luna interrupted, her face hardening.

I know, but I still want to be with you. Can you give us a chance? Just for tonight, and then you'll never see me again.

"I love you," Alan whispered, stroking her cheek with his thumb.

"I love you too," she whispered while grasping his hands.

Alan leaned forward for a kiss. She closed her eyes and accepted it. Alan's hands traveled from her hair to her shoulders. Luna placed her hands around his neck and deepened her kiss. Alan lingered on her soft shoulders and slowly slid his hands to her waist. Luna shivered with pleasure and then pulled away.

"Should we go somewhere more private?" she asked, rubbing his chest. Alan felt eagerness rising. *There was no way that this was happening,* he thought.

"I mean, if you want to," she said coyly.

"Yes," Alan answered, trying not to vomit from his insides twisting from nervousness. He led Luna to the guest bedroom and pushed her on the bed. She let out a giggle and continued to kiss him. His insides were throbbing, and he pulled down the sleeves of her dress, exposing her shoulders and chest. He gently kissed her neck and shoulders. Taking in her scent. They embraced, entangled in love.

Chapter 15

WITH FRIENDS LIKE THESE

Luna was in heaven, arching her back. She felt Alan tense up and then grip the bed sheets next to her head. He grunted and then relaxed on top of her. Luna went from delighted to horrified.

"Did you just finish?" she whispered in Alan's ear, even though she already knew the answer. Alan sat up. Sweat poured down his flushed face, and he still tried to catch his breath.

"Sorry," he huffed and rested his head on her chest. "You were too good," he mumbled into her cleavage. Rage surged through Luna, and she swatted his face.

You ass! "You said you were going to pull out," she hissed. She wanted to strangle him but knew deep down that wouldn't change anything.

"Ow," he moaned and rolled off her.

Luna heard footsteps down the hallway.

"I thought you said no one was home," she told Alan, furrowing her brow. Alan shot up and pulled on his shirt.

154

"We have to hide you," he whispered and helped her off the bed. Luna trembled while looking for a place to escape around the room. The door swung open, and a muscular man with sandy blond hair gaped at them. Alan's face went beet red. They stood frozen in shock.

The man closed the door but remained outside. Tears streamed down Luna's face.

"What we do," she whimpered. "He'll report me, and they'll kill me," she sobbed. She felt foolish and terrified. Alan wiped her tears away.

It'll be okay. "I'm going to talk to him," he soothed. "Clean yourself up in the bathroom, and I'll come get you," he instructed and pointed to a small door in the bedroom. She didn't believe him, but what choice did she have? Luna grabbed her undergarments from the floor and ran into the bathroom. She locked it and slid to the ground.

She hugged her knees and buried her face into her chest. Warm tears streamed down her face, and she pressed her lips together to suppress her sobs. Memories of Darnelle being carried away in handcuffs came to her. She imagined Beatrice's hurt expression and her mother wailing at her after discovering what she had done. She was overcome with distraught and wished to fade into the floor. To escape the dreadful predicament that she had put herself in. Her thoughts were interrupted by Alan and the man arguing in the other room. Luna took a few deep breaths to calm her nerves and pressed her ear against the door.

"Who is that?" the man interrogated.

"Just a friend," Alan shrugged.

Since when do you bang your friends?

"I did no such thing," Alan denied.

Alan, I'm not fucking stupid! "I walk in here, and you guys are half naked," the man yelled. Is she even allowed up here? She doesn't like anyone from the Cloud or Star sector.

"It's fine; she has her Day Pass," Alan replied.

Why would she need a day pass? Wait, is she below floor 75?

"No," Alan lied.

Okay, then, where is she from?

Alan didn't answer. Luna pressed her ear closer to the door and concentrated hard.

She heard Alan yelp in pain.

"Where is she from?" the man growled.

"Ocean," Alan mumbled. A tense silence hung in the air.

"That's gross, man," the man snarled. I know you don't get much action, but you don't do that.

It's weird.

"Why do you care?" Alan protested.

Oh, I don't… But mom will.

"You wouldn't," Alan retorted, his voice oozed with fear. It would literally kill her.

"I can and will," the man sneered. If I need to.

"What will it take for you to keep this between us?" Alan bargained. I'll do anything. I'll pay you anything. "Just please, I need you to keep this to yourself," Alan begged.

The man paused.

"Introduce me to your plug," he commanded. I need more Gush.

Gush? Luna thought to herself, and her stomach dropped. "Alan, No," she breathed at the realization.

Okay. "Okay, I will," Alan agreed. Just leave us.

Luna heard the door slam and footsteps recede down the hallway. Luna cleaned herself up and washed her face. She sat back down at the front of the door, unable to face Alan. He had deceived her and lied about it. *What could have caused him to do this? Could she trust him anymore?* She felt stupid for letting herself be vulnerable. She should have listened to Beatrice, but it was too late.

A soft knock at the door pulled her attention. She apprehensively opened the door and faced Alan.

Sorry about my brother Logan.

"He's going to keep what happened tonight to himself, so you should be safe," Alan said, adjusting his glasses.

"Why?" she whispered.

Why, what?

"Why are you working with Hoodi?" Luna flared.

I- Alan started.

"Don't try to lie," Luna cried. Your brother said something about Gush, and Hoodi is the only one who sells it. So, why are you working with him when you said you wouldn't?

"I needed the money for your Day Pass," he admitted. I wanted you to be happy and be with me.

Luna's eyes watered, and she looked away.

I've stopped. I promise. I did it because I love you, please don't be upset.

"You loving me doesn't excuse your actions and going against your word," Luna sobbed. You've put us in more danger than you realize. Hoodi will use me to blackmail you to get what he wants. To control you. "You could love me all you want, but I don't trust you," Luna whimpered and stepped back.

"Luna-" Alan trembled and tried to grab her hand. Rage and pain radiated through her body, but she didn't want to say anything she would regret later. So, she took in a shaky breath.

"It's just been a bad night," Luna croaked, pulling away her hand. I want to go home.

Alan looked as if she had struck him.

"Okay," he whispered.

Alan led her to the elevator. The air between them was heavy and tense. I'm sorry for everything that happened tonight.

"Can you forgive me, please?" he pleaded as she entered the elevator. Luna glared at him and said nothing. She was hurt by his dishonesty and still humiliated by his brother barging in on them. She didn't have the strength to speak. All she wanted to do was cry in solitude.

"Will I see you again?" he asked weakly, hurt etched in his face.

Luna stood in silence as the elevator slammed shut.

***

Alan sat in silence and stared at his desk table clock. The red number 4:00 reflected at him. He couldn't sleep. Luna's pain-stricken expression haunted him. He wanted to chase after her, to explain his side of the story and beg for forgiveness. However, keeping his brother quiet was the more pressing matter. Alan never considered himself to be an aggressive person, but when Logan walked through that door, he wanted to punch his brother in the face. They had never been close, but this was their first time they argued about something. Alan was also concerned about his brother's desperation to get Gush. Maybe his brother was developing an addiction.

Alan pulled up Hoodi's contact on his phone. He sent Hoodi a message to try to meet up again, but Hoodi read the message and never responded. He and Logan might have to physically find him in the Ocean Sector. *Where would be the best place to start?* He read through his previous messages with Hoodi. He noticed that Hoodi mentioned a person named Harold as a contact point to wash the money before changing the plan to donate the money to the house.

Harold could help him find Hoodi. Alan tried to strategize how he would approach Harold and convince Hoodi to work with his obnoxious brother. However, his mind kept drifting to Luna. Her kind eyes, her soft skin, and her sweet laugh. His heart ached at the thought of hurting her, of her rejecting him. He slowly descended into a restless slumber.

Alan awakened with a jolt as cold water was poured onto his face. Logan was towering over him with a cup and a wicked smile.

"Mornin' asshole," his brother bellowed and pinched his side.

Alan let out a frustrated sigh and rubbed his face.

"Logan, what do you want?" Alan groaned and put on his glasses.

"For you to uphold your promise," Logan said.

"Oh yeah," Alan moaned and made his way out of the bed.

"So, when are we going to meet your supplier?" Logan demanded while rubbing his hands together.

I'm not sure yet. He hasn't answered my messages. We could talk to one of his contacts and arrange a meeting.

"Are you okay with going to the Ocean Sector tonight after my classes?" Alan inquired while pulling out a change of clothes.

"Yeah, yeah, that shouldn't be a problem," Logan confirmed, scratching his arm.

Don't worry. I'll message you.

"I just hope he answers back," Alan said, checking his phone.

"Yeah, yeah," Logan mumbled and cleared his throat.

"So, uhh, what was it like?" Logan asked.

"What was, what like?" Alan mocked in irritation. He didn't like where the conversation was going. So, I just want to clarify that I think your taste is kind of weird and freaky. And I would have never expected you to be into people like her, but I gotta ask.

Okayyyy… Alan said apprehensively.

"So, is her pussy sideways?" Logan inquired, his expression serious. Cause I heard from my boy Tony, the girls down there are like that.

"I'm not into that, of course," Logan defended. I just wanted to know.

Alan watched a smirk cross his brother's face and realized he was trying to get a reaction out of him. He also knew that his brother would keep bothering him until he answered.

"Uhhh, it's normal," Alan replied, hoping his brother would leave.

"Ha, I knew it," Logan proclaimed and grinned as if he just won a bet.

"You also might want to see a doctor," Logan continued.

Why?

So, I heard from Tony that his friend's cousin slept with an ocean girl, and his dick turned black and fell off.

I just care about you, bro.

Alan stifled a snort. *Why is my brother so dumb?* he thought to himself.

"I'm sure I'll be fine," Alan reassured.

"You need to stop listening to your friend Tony. All that matters is you don't tell Mom. She can't handle it. Remember when she panicked because the white dish towels she ordered were yellow? "It would destroy her," Alan reminded him, hoping this would change the conversation.

"Yeah, yeah," Logan replied dismissively. I'll see you later. "Stay out of trouble," Logan motioned to Alan and departed.

Alan rolled his eyes. Bringing his brother to Hoodi was going to be a nightmare.

Alan changed into his university uniform and made his way to class. He sat at the very top of the auditorium and pretended to take notes. Occasionally flattening his gray suit and brushing off lent. The professor, an old man with large spectacles, continued to drone on and on about balancing accounts. Across the auditorium, he noticed two of Logan's friends whispering and laughing at him. It dawned on Alan. He told his brother that he couldn't say anything to his parents. This didn't include other people. His brother probably shared what happened with some of his friends. He would have to clarify when he got home.

Alan didn't relish the negative attention. At the end of the lesson, he got up and rushed out of the study hall.

Alan threw his textbooks on the bed and stormed towards Logan's bedroom. He banged on the door, fighting anger and trepidation towards his brother.

"Come in," Logan broadcasted. Alan opened the door and was greeted by blue smoke and loud music. Logan snorted a line of stardust on a metal pan at his computer desk and rubbed his nose.

"Hey, you ready to go," Logan boomed, taking a drag from his vape.

"Ava, turn off the music," Alan yelled.

"Turning off," a woman's voice chimed, and the music paused.

"I'm ready, but I want to clarify something," Alan said.

What?

Make sure you don't tell anyone about Luna and me, not just mom. "Remember, we don't want to upset or bring any shame to our parents," Alan explained.

Right.... Right, Logan nodded. Sorry, I might have mentioned it to Tony.

"Just tell him you were joking," Alan suggested.

"But then I would lose the argument," Logan whined.

"Come on, man," Alan groaned and raked his hands in frustration.

"Hey, my lips are sealed," Logan said, holding up his hands.

Alan let out a sigh of relief.

"So her name's Luna," Logan noted with a devious expression.

Alan glared at him and said nothing. It was taking everything in his power not to knock the patronizing expression off his face.

"That woman must have you in a choke hold," Logan muttered in amusement.

"Come on, let's go," Alan motioned to the exit. He refused to explain himself to anyone, especially Logan, of all people.

***

An orchestra bathed in red light sat on the stage. They strummed on large wooden instruments and filled the dance hall with notes filled with jazz undertones. Several patrons held lit cigarettes, creating a haze in the dance hall that burned Alan's nose. They chatted in hushed voices and wore tattered old clothes.

"Goddard, bring me a beverage," Logan broadcasted as they moved between the black-clothed tables.

A few of the members glanced up in curiosity. Then, they quickly looked away, frantically whispering to each other in fear.

"They don't have any goddards down here," Alan mumbled in annoyance. We are below floor 50, remember.

What? No Goddards. "Then how am I supposed to get a drink," Logan exclaimed.

Alan shushed him.

"Just follow my lead," Alan pleaded.

Did you just shush me?

"No one shushes me," Logan boomed in anger.

"Hey, look, I'm sorry," Alan whispered, trying to calm his brother down. But we gotta keep our voices down. We don't want to bring any attention to ourselves.

"The dealer wants us to be discreet," Alan explained.

Got it. "Right!" Logan agreed.

Alan let out a sigh and led them to the bar.

The venue seemed calmer than the fundraiser event Luna invited him to, and Alan was thankful. He wanted Logan and him to be as inconspicuous as possible. A bald man with a purple beard and golden chain was mixing drinks at the bar. As Logan and Alan sat at the bar, the other customers next to them scowled and moved to one of the tables facing the band. The man made eye contact with them, and Alan recognized him as Carl. The person who took his donation at the charity event. Carl wore blue lipstick, and a Hawaiian blue feather dangled from his ear. Carl approached them and wore a despondent expression.

"What can I do for you, gentlemen, this evening?" Carl greeted. Alan motioned for him to come forward.

"We have a message for Harold," Alan whispered into Carl's ear. It's important.

"In regards to what?" Carl drawled.

Alan checked his surroundings before continuing.

"Hoodi," he whispered. Carl raised his eyebrows.

"Follow me," he drawled and led them towards the back of the room.

Carl knocked three times on a section of the wall and then pushed it open. Behind the wall was a stairwell that led to a plain door labeled *office*. Alan thanked Carl, and then they began to ascend the stairs. Carl nodded and shut the wall panel behind him. Alan entered a cramped office with several books and papers piled haphazardly around an aged wooden desk. An old man with silver spectacles looked up at them in confusion.

"Hi, are you Harold?" Alan croaked in apprehension.

Yes, who sent you?

We are working with Hoodi.

The old man jumped up and knelt in front of their feet. Fat tears streamed down his wrinkled face, and black hair flowed wildly around the bald spot on the top of his head.

Please!

"Please tell Hoodi to have mercy on me," he begged. I only need three more days before I can pay him back.

"Please don't hurt my family," he sobbed into the floor. Alan and Logan looked at each other bewildered. This was not what Alan had expected.

"We aren't going to hurt you," he reassured the feeble old man as he helped him up. Harold wiped his tears away and stifled a few sniffs.

"So, what does Hoodi want then?" Harold inquired.

So, we don't speak for Hoodi.

"We just work with him by moving some products to the Star Sector," Alan explained.

"We were hoping to arrange a meeting with him about getting some more supplies," Logan interjected.

"So, you came to me?" Harold asked and held out his hands in confusion.

"He wasn't answering my messages and mentioned you as a point of contact," Alan continued.

We just want to talk to him.

"I see," Harold blinked. So, he usually gets here around eleven to check in with other dealers and do business in the Twilight room.

"If you feel comfortable waiting around that long, you could make your proposal," Harold suggested.

"Are you okay with that?" Alan asked Logan.

"With enough drinks, I can wait all night," Logan beamed.

"I like this guy," Harold said, giving Logan a firm handshake.

"So, I need to know," Harold continued.

How do you know about me from Hoodi?

Alan hesitated.

He felt he could be honest with Harold. The man just cried in front of him and begged for his life.

"He wanted me to give you some money to wash," Alan admitted. Harold's face brightened.

"Oh, you're the one who made that huge donation during the charity event," Harold affirmed.

"Yes," Alan admitted and adjusted his glasses. Harold paused in deep thought.

Can I ask you an honest question?

Yes.

"Why are you working with Hoodi?" You two don't look like you are in desperate need of money.

Alan blushed while Logan grinned.

"I think it was for his ocean lady," Logan said and nudged his brother.

Alan scowled and pushed him back. Harold's expression darkened.

"Oh, please elaborate," Harold growled, eyes boring into Alan.

I... "I just needed the money to get a Day Pass for a close friend of mine," Alan sputtered.

A friend, huh?

"Yes, the lovely Miss Luna," Logan jeered. Alan shot Logan a spiteful look.

"What?" his brother mouthed back.

"Oh my god, you're him," Harold moaned, realization crossing his leathery face. "I've heard a great deal about you," he said, shaking his head.

You've been giving my B a lot of grief. "That girl is like a daughter to her," Harold continued. Alan's blush deepened, and he was lost for words.

Logan looked at both men in confusion.

I… Alan started.

"Save it," Harold snapped and held his hand up. I've seen this a thousand times. And it ends the same way every time. You won't be the first, and you won't be the last.

"But why work with someone like Hoodi?" Harold inquired.

"He seemed okay," Alan trailed off.

Harold groaned in concern. It seems you don't know him well. But how could you? You're so far away from us. "You haven't had a chance to see the terror he evokes down here," Harold eluded cryptically.

"Hey, look, old man," Logan interjected. We just need to talk with him about getting more pills. There won't be any issues.

The old man eyed them and then let out a small laugh. "I see you have the situation under control," he remarked. Please make yourself comfortable and make sure to steer clear of the neon bar. "I think if my

B sees you, she might attack," Harold mentioned, looking up at Alan.

Alan shifted uncomfortably. I'll bring drinks to you in the Twilight room. Talk to Carl if you need anything else. Alan thanked him, and they made their way down the staircase.

Chapter 16

SCAPEGOAT

"I feel so stupid," Luna sobbed into Safari's lap.

"You're not stupid," Safari soothed, gently stroking her hair. He's the one who deceived you. You were just vulnerable with him, and he took advantage. It happens more than you think.

"What if I get pregnant?" Luna cried as tears glided down her terror-stricken face. My mother... Beatrice, they'll hate me. "They won't ever speak to me again," Luna whimpered and pressed her face into Safari's dress.

"You don't know that yet," Safari reassured, handing her friend a tissue. There's no need to despair.

"Do you hate me?" Luna squeaked between sobs.

No, I could never hate you. "But I think you've made quite a mess of things, and unfortunately, these things aren't going to go away any time soon," Safari continued. But crying isn't going to help or change anything that's happened.

171

Luna looked up at her friend. She knew Safari was providing sound advice. She whipped her face and stood up.

"You're right," she sniffed. "I'm just scared," Luna breathed. He's working with Hoodi. Hoodi will surely come after me when things go wrong. And I have nowhere to run or hide. "I feel trapped," Luna cried, sitting back on the bed.

You're right. You can't run or hide. "So what's left to do?" Safari asked and held her friend's hand.

Luna shook her head in frustration.

"I'm not brave like you," Luna trembled and squeezed her hand. I'm not a fighter. Never had been.

"I think when push comes to shove, you will," Safari remarked. Luna embraced her friend and buried her face in her shoulder, releasing soft sobs. Safari patted her back in an attempt to comfort her friend.

Delta pushed open the door, her red dress elegantly flowing into the room.

"Is she still crying?" Delta snarled, digging her crimson claws into the doorway in irritation.

"No, she's getting herself together," Safari said, giving her friend an encouraging look.

Luna dried her eyes with the crumpled-up tissue. "Would you be willing to give us a few more moments?" Luna begged.

We can't just sit around here like rotting bags of meat. "There is work to be done," Deta blazed.

The house will leave in five minutes.

Delta turned, her golden earring glinting in the hallway light, and departed.

You heard mother. "Let's get ready," Safari asserted, patting Luna's leg. Safari drifted to the closet and rummaged through the intricate costumes that filled the small space.

Luna pushed her anguish to the side and sat in front of the mirror. Her face was puffy, and her eyes were ruddy from crying. She picked up the shell-encrusted brush and pulled the bristles through her curls. The sensation calmed her and brought back pleasant memories of her mother brushing her hair. Safari brought her two dresses and laid them on the bed. She held up a mermaid dress with golden sequins rippling through ruby lace.

What do you think of this one?

"What's the category?" Luna inquired.

No category. We are just watching the Struts perform tonight.

"Oh, I would wear something more casual," Luna replied. Safari switched it out with the other dress and put it on. The black dress flared out at her knees and wrist.

"Ooo, it's giving 60s fantasy," Luna chirped, admiring the silhouette.

"I'll put on my hoop earrings then," Safari vocalized and walked back into the closet.

Luna took in her surroundings. The water-stained paper peeled from the wall. The cold concrete floor had drops of condensation on it. The faded sheets and dull yellow light covered the dreary room. It had been familiar, her home. Yet, after experiencing the splendor of the Star Sector, her home felt suffocating. She felt guilty. She should be grateful that she got the opportunity to see the wealthy city. However, she wanted to go back and see the stars again. Her mind drifted to Alan, and then she wrecked with sorrow all over again.

She took in a deep breath to suppress another sob. Even though Safari was her best friend, she could tell her friend was growing weary of her tears and hearing about him. Luna didn't want to be alone. She needed distraction.

"Can I come with you?" she asked, turning to her friend.

"If Mother allows it," Safari replied, putting on her earrings. Luna admired her reflection and continued brushing her hair.

***

Alan took another drag from the metallic owl and rehearsed what he would say to Hoodi. Logan sat beside him, slouched over the bench, letting green smoke coming out of his mouth. They were in the same room as when Alan met Hoodi for the first time, but it was less crowded. Muffled jazz music emanated from the wall, and people in dirty costumes lazily inhaled the smoke.

"This stuff isn't as smooth as Quartz," Logan coughed and put the tube back on the table.

"Well, it's probably made of cheaper ingredients," Alan stated, running his hands through his hair.

Do you want me to get you a drink?

"Nah, I just want to get Gush and leave this dump," Logan yawned and put his feet on the table.

So, what's this guy like anyway?

"He's interesting," Alan said. I need you to be on your best behavior, okay? After talking to Harold, I don't want to piss this guy off.

"Yeah, yeah," Logan mumbled dismissively, placing his hands behind his head.

A blond man with sparkly cowboy boots and jean shorts approached them. His chest rippled underneath a fishnet shirt, flexing several tattoos and muscles. He wore the a bright pink cowboy hat and a feather dangled from his left ear.

"How are you fellas doing?" Hoodi broadcasted, his blue eyes twinkling in the pale light. Three men in black sweatshirts with pink triangles in the center appeared behind him. Their faces were shrouded with pink masks and upside-down black triangles. The men made Alan uneasy, but Logan lifted his head, entertained by the bizarre group in front of him.

"Alan, you didn't say we would be visiting fairies today," Logan laughed.

Hoodi's smile faded, and he sat in front of the table. The three hooded men followed and stood behind him with their hands on their backs.

"Alan, who did you bring with you tonight?" Hoodi asked, studying Logan.

"It's Logan," Logan interrupted. So, let's just get to the point. I've already wasted enough time here.

"Alan and I want another shipment of Gush," Logan demanded.

Alan flinched at his brother's crass demands. This was going a lot worse than he anticipated.

He's pretty direct. "Isn't he?" Hoodi commented, looking over at Alan.

"So, do we have a deal or not?" Logan inquired, a smirk spreading over his face.

Hoodi ignored him and kept his attention on Alan. His face was granite. Alan's stomach bubbled with nervousness.

"Tell your idiot brother I'm not interested," Hoodi asserted. Logan leaped off the bench and grabbed Hoodi's shirt.

"You want to say to my face, asshole," Logan snarled and yanked Hoodi forward.

"Ooo, not too hard, Daddy," Hoodi moaned and flashed Logan his yellow teeth.

Logan recoiled, and the henchmen roared with laughter.

"What my brother means to say is we want to keep doing business," Alan piped up and held his hand up to keep his brother back.

But you told me last week you wanted out. "What changed?" Hoodi inquired, shifting his attention back to Alan.

I.."I just need more money," Alan lied. You know Alan.

"You are not a good liar," Hoodi observed. I think others are pressuring you to do things you aren't invested in. Alan averted his gaze and looked at the floor.

"So, do we have a deal, right?" Logan pressed. His voice grew in desperation.

Alan, a deal is a deal. "You said you wanted out, so

I'm going to respect that," Hoodi continued. He stood up and made his way out.

"I'll report you," Logan threatened, his fist clenching.

Will you stop? He's not interested," Alan hissed, trying to hold Logan back. Logan pulled away from him and scowled. Hoodi turned around, pulled out a Barbie pink pistol from his shorts, and aimed it at Logan. The three men behind him assembled machine guns. Many of the guests hid under tables or scuffled out of the room. Logan and Alan held their hands up in surrender.

Alan gulped, and Logan breathed hard. Hoodi clicked the safety off his pistol.

"Report what?" Hoodi inquired, mincing his teeth. The air was still and silent.

"Forget it," Logan muttered.

"Oh, don't worry, I'll make sure of that," Hoodi declared and fired his pistol.

Alan dropped to the floor while Logan cried out in pain and gripped his arm. Blood oozed from the gunshot womb. "Make sure they get the message," Hoodie ordered his henchmen. The three cloaked individuals descended on them. Alan curled into a ball as he felt fists bruise his body and boots stomp on his limbs. *This is the end*, he thought to himself, blood trickled down his face.

He closed his eyes and thought of his family and Luna's radiant face. The fists receded as he heard shouting and boots pounding on the ground. Alan weakly opened his eyes and saw a tall black woman with red hair pointing a gun at Hoodi. Behind her were five people dressed in black with red boots. Alan vaguely remembered them from Beatrice's charity event. Alan's eyes locked on Luna, who contrasted with the other members and dressed in the purple. They all aimed guns at Hoodi, except for Luna, who hid behind a woman with orange braids.

"This has nothing to do with you," Hoodi growled, now pointing his gun at the woman. The woman placed her hand on her hip and scowled at him.

You're disturbing the peace at my favorite establishment," the woman quipped. So, yes, it does deal with me. Here, I am trying to enjoy a refreshing beverage with my family, and a wanna-be cowboy without style booty shorts is shooting up the Twilight room.

"Ooooo," two of the men chanted, snapping their fingers. Tell him, mother.

Hoodi opened his mouth to retort but was cut off by the fiery woman.

"This is not the time or place for such tomfoolery," she continued. It's time for you and your washed-up followers to leave. Goodbye. Hoodi glared at her and put his gun back into his shorts.

"This isn't over," he declared, waving his finger in her face.

"Let's go, fellas," he commanded. He and the other henchmen disappeared into the jazz club.

Luna rushed over to Alan, her face full of concern.

"Are you all right?" she asked and handed him his cracked glasses.

"I'm doing better now," Alan croaked and put the glasses back on.

"Boris, get me a towel," the woman demanded and put away her gun. A man with a velvet blue tuxedo rushed in with a dish towel.

Gina, go ahead and try to stop the bleeding.

"Safari and Henry, go ahead and let Beatrice know what happened," the woman ordered. Gina pressed the towel against Logan's gunshot womb while the other members scattered. The woman approached Alan, her face hard and angry.

"Look what a mess you've made," she scolded. I know you think you're better off than us lower-floor folk, but that doesn't give you the right to disrupt our establishment.

Alan sat up. He was terrified of the woman but glad she stepped in when she did.

"Thank you for saving us," he told the woman. The woman's face softened.

"I like this one," she said to Luna, pointing at him. He's got good manners. Luna beamed at him. Alan's heart melted.

"Well, my work is done," the woman sniffed. "Children, let us go back to enjoying our strawberry daiquiris," the woman commanded and marched out of the room. The other members followed, except for Luna, who held Alan's hand. They gazed at each other for a few moments. Luna tried to stand up, but Alan gripped her hand.

"I'm sorry for everything," he confessed, holding her hand tighter. Luna had her breath and cast her attention on the bruises on his arm.

"You got lucky Delta stepped in when she did," Luna continued, looking over at Logan, who was scowling at both of them.

Come on, let's get you guys home. Luna helped Logan, and Alan got up on his own.

"Can I see, please?" she asked, encouraging him to remove the towel.

I want to make sure you don't bleed out. Logan pulled off the towel and winced in pain.

"You got lucky," Luna said while studying the injury. It looks like the bullet just grazed your skin.

You should only need a few stitches.

"Should he go to the hospital?" Alan questioned, his concern for his brother growing.

"The closest hospital is on floor 25," Luna replied. "People get treatments at doctor's offices here, but it isn't super sanitary," Luna noted.

"Screw that," Logan shouted. I'm going home. Luna helped Logan get into the elevator, and they both ascended upwards.

"I can only take you to 50," she said, her voice empty. "Do you think you can get him home?"

Alan nodded and took over. The three of them exited into the Land Sector rest stop.

"I guess this is goodbye then," Luna whispered and pushed her hair back her ear. Alan wanted to keep talking to her, reconnecting and being friends again, but he had to tend to his brother.

Yeah.

"Tell Delta thank you again for me," Alan said and waved goodbye.

"Oh my god, you two are going to make me vomit," Logan complained as they ascended to the next sector.

"Why?" Alan replied apathetically and looked over at his brother. You guys were awkwardly flirting with each other while I was bleeding from my gunshot womb.

I don't know what you mean. I was being polite. "Which was the opposite of what you were doing. You were being rude and aggressive with Hoodi," Alan argued.

First of all, it's called negotiating. I was not aggressive at all. Second of all, how was I supposed to know he was going to pull a gun on us? He looks like a gay Ken doll. "What self-respecting drug dealer wears booty shorts, anyway," Logan complained.

Alan let out a weak laugh. For once, he and his brother agreed on something. "Yeah, he's a character," Alan trailed off.

Alan and Logan entered the last elevator. Alan was relieved that he was almost home.

"What's so special about that girl anyway?" Logan demanded, breaking the silence.

"Why do you care?" Alan muttered, looking up at the ceiling.

I don't, but I notice you turn into an even bigger drooling idiot around her. "She's cute but also fat, so that makes her like an automatic three," Logan continued.

" It's more than just looks," Alan replied, trying to suppress his irritation. She and I have a lot in common: she's kind and laughs at all my jokes. "And in case you haven't noticed, I'm not exactly skinny," Alan motioned to his body.

"Yeah, but that only applies to girls," Logan continued in a bored tone.

"Man, you're so shallow," Alan laughed. I don't expect you or mom or dad to understand.

"Why's that?" Logan sneered.

Everything we do is performative as if we have to be part of a picture-perfect family. I don't even want to be an accountant, but I have to be one because it makes good money. I hate the people we meet at these giant dinner parties, and I have to pretend I like them. I have the same conversation over and over again about the weather. I'm just tired of it all. With her, I don't have to be fake. "I can be myself," Alan confessed.

"Wow, man," Logan said and patted his back. "Do you want me to hold your purse now?" Logan jeered.

Alan rolled his eyes. He knew that was his brother's way of saying, *I understand*. It didn't make him feel any less annoyed.

Logan and Alan stepped into Floor 155, which was the hospital wing for the Star Sector. Goddards wheeled several patients in and out of an arch doorway with a glowing red emergency sign above it. Alan led them to the front desk, where a nurse styled her nails.

"Grab a clipboard and go to room 23," she said in a raspy voice. She didn't look up from her nails. Alan grabbed a clipboard and arrived at the room. He knocked on the door, and a white Goddard with a stethoscope greeted them.

"Please have a seat, gentlemen," it buzzed. Logan sat on the bed while Alan sat on the chair. A red probe appeared on Goddard's head, and Alan and Logan were scanned.

"Computing," it beeped and projected a hologram from its chest. You have minor injuries displayed on the screen. Would you like treatment? If so, please press submit.

Logan laid down on the bed, and Alan pressed the submit button. A bright yellow light illuminated above Logan. It swept past him, healing all the bruises and the gunshot womb. Logan stretched and slinked off the couch. Alan switched places with him, and Logan pressed the submit button. After the healing laser covered Alan, his aching body felt immediate relief. He analyzed his arms, and the bruises and cuts disappeared. Gunpowder residue was found on your body, sir.

"Would you like to file a police report?" the goddard buzzed at Logan.

"Yes, I would," Logan remarked with a smug expression.

Alan frowned at him and left the room. He fulfilled his part of the bargain and refused to participate in Logan's scheme against Hoodi.

***

"Oh no, what happened?" Luna cried, scanning the room. The ballroom looked like a tornado had hit it. Tables and chairs were upside down or snapped in half. Broken glass and trash littered the floor. The Ocean Sector tapestries and artwork were shredded and scattered over the concrete floor.

"It looks like Hoodi's trying to send us a message," Beatrice huffed and pointed to the pink triangle spray-painted on the wall.

"I feel like this is somehow my fault," Luna confessed. She secretly wondered if Alan had a role in destroying the bar.

"It's not your fault, my dear," Beatrice drawled and sat on one of the unbroken bar stools. It's my husband's. He invited that monster in here.

"What choice did I have?" Harold cried from behind the bar. We were so behind on our bills B. "We would have lost everything," he argued, waving his arms around.

"We have lost everything," Beatrice remarked bitterly. Look around you. "This will take months to repair, and just when things were getting better," she sighed.

Luna placed her hand on Beatrice's back. "Don't worry, I'll help you clean up," Luna said. She wanted to tell Beatrice that things would get better, but Beatrice's defeated expression told her she wasn't in the mood for her positivity. Beatrice grunted but didn't move.

Luna grabbed a broom and started sweeping the broken glass into a pile. The image of Alan covered in bruises and his broken glasses came to mind. She silently hoped they were safe and got treatment for their injuries. She also wondered if Hoodi would go after them. She rationalized it was unlikely due to both living in a wealthier sector and felt better.

Three police officers wearing star sector uniforms walked in. Luna looked over at Harold.

"Did you call them?" she mouthed to Harold. Harold shook his head, and the color drained from his face.

"Can we please speak to the owner of this establishment?" the officer in front commanded.

"I'm here," Beatrice sighed and crossed her arms.

So at 12:35 am last night, we got reports that a citizen from the Star Sector was shot here.

Is that correct?

Beatrice hesitated, and Luna gripped the broom tightly.

Yes, but... Beatrice started.

"You are under arrest for the assault of a star citizen," the officer announced. The second officer pulled her hands behind her back while the third-placed her in handcuffs. Luna's heart dropped. She knew Beatrice's arrest was unjust, but she could do nothing to stop it. Beatrice's face twisted in outrage, and she started to squirm.

"Don't fight it, B," Harold told her. Don't fight.

Beatrice stopped squirming, but her face remained hard. She and the other two officers left the ballroom. The officer who ordered her arrest was typing into a tablet.

"Excuse me," Luna squeaked, slowly approaching the officer. She flinched at the nightstick around his waist. Unpleasant memories of being beaten by one surfaced. She blinked them away, trying to find the courage to talk to the officer.

"May I ask why Beatrice is being taken in?" Luna asked, trying to keep her expression soft and demure.

"We got a report that a citizen was shot on this floor and then an anonymous tip that she was the one who did it," the officer sniffed dismissively. *Hoodi,* Luna thought to herself. "We are taking her to the jail on floor 2," the officer continued. Here is information about bail and her arrest if you need it. The officer handed Luna a ticket and continued typing on his tablet. She thanked the officer and analyzed the ticket. It was suspiciously empty. A lot of the information was missing. Luna went over to Harold, who was in a puddle of tears.

"My B... they took my B," he sobbed. I can't without my B.

Luna wrapped her arms around the trembling old man and checked to ensure the officer left.

Harold. "Harold, look, this is important," Luna whispered, holding out the ticket.

Harold took a few deep breaths and studied the ticket.

"This seems off," he said, furrowing his brow.

"I think Hoodi's behind this," Luna continued. The officer said that they were arresting her over an anonymous tip after a report was made. So, I bet Hoodi tried to shift the blame to Beatrice with the anonymous tip.

"Or Hoodi paid them off," Harold grumbled. It doesn't matter. "We would need a good lawyer to clear her name," he sighed. And we're just buried under so much debt. He took off his glasses and wiped his shirt with them.

"We can't give up yet," Luna said. We both have to right this wrong. "For B," she cried. Harold sniffed and nodded. Luna grabbed the broom and started sweeping again. As she aided Harold with fixing the bar, she wracked her brain on how to save Beatrice and bring Hoodi to justice.

Chapter 17

GREAT EXPECTATIONS

Luna let out a frustrated sigh as she could not button up her pants. This was the third pair she tried this morning, and none would fit. She studied her reflection and placed her hand on her swollen belly. She hadn't changed her diet, so why was she gaining so much weight? She thought hard, and a chill ran down her spine. She couldn't remember the last time she had her period. Luna didn't want to admit it, but she was worried she might be pregnant. She switched into sweatpants, and her low abdomen continued to protrude. She also put on a sweatshirt, hoping it would better hide her stomach.

Luna made her way out of the apartment and climbed up a tube that led to the closest convenience store. A bell chimed as she entered the store. A slim selection of products was displayed on the shelf. Fruit and vegetables were bruised and wrinkled. The shelves were covered in dust. Mrs. Ang, an old Asian woman, was napping behind the counter with her arms crossed. Luna made her way to the hygiene section of the store. She spotted a pregnancy test on the counter, wedged between toothpaste and pads. A part of her wanted to slip it into her sweatshirt to hide her embarrassment, but she could feel Mrs. Ang's eyes on her. Luna picked up the pregnancy test and brought it to the counter.

"Do you need a bag?" Mrs. Ang drawled.

"Yes, please," Luna replied, averting her gaze. Mrs. Ang paused but said nothing and placed the test into the bag.

"Good luck," Mrs. Ang waved. Luna clutched the bag and departed.

Luna anxiously sat on the toilet, holding the pregnancy test. *Please be negative,* she begged. *Please.* She checked the back of the box to ensure she followed the instructions correctly. A pink plus sign appeared on the test. Tears hit the green tile floor in her bathroom, and she angrily threw the test towards the trash bin. She buried her face into her hands and was paralyzed in fear. Her mind raced. *How do I tell mom? Should I tell Alan? I'm not ready to be a mother.* A loud knock on the door interrupted her sobs.

"Luna, it's 7 you're going to be late," her mother called. Luna placed her hand over her mouth to stifle her cries. She wiped her eyes and tried to steady her voice.

"Okay," she replied, hiding the test at the bottom of the trash bin.

"Maybe it's a false positive," Luna told herself. She would have to do another test after work. She washed her face and rushed to the transportation elevator. Luna joined the masses of workers heading to the Tilapia plant. Safari greeted her and yawned.

"Morning, lady, are you feeling okay?" Safari inquired.

Yes, of course. "Why do you ask?" Luna replied, facing forward.

You look pale and sweaty. And you're wearing sweatpants again.

"Yeah, I just have an upset stomach," Luna lied. She wanted to tell her friend about the test and express how terrified she felt. However, she wanted to confirm she was pregnant before admitting it to anyone.

"Hey, what's wrong with you?" Safari pressed and placed a fish into a cardboard box.

Nothing. "Nothing's wrong," Luna said hotly, and she passed the next fish to her.

You seem withdrawn today. Usually, you would be talking my ear off, but you're so quiet.

I…" I just don't feel well," Luna huffed and passed down another fish.

Any way I can help? Luna paused and was tempted to blurt out what happened, but too many people could overhear.

"Do you have any plans tonight?" Luna croaked.

No plans. Would you be willing to hang out with me?

"Sure," Safari agreed, bringing her attention back to her work. Luna was thankful to have her as a friend.

***

"I can't look," Luna moaned, holding her head in her hand and handing Safari the pregnancy test. Safari looked grave.

"It's positive," she informed her and handed it back. Luna sat in silence, lost in thought. Safari placed her hand on her back.

"You have options, you know," Safari said gently. I know.

"I just can't," Luna replied, placing her hand on her stomach.

"You need to tell him then," Safari pressed.

I know. I just don't know how. I've been so busy trying to help Beatrice. "We haven't talked in a while," Luna explained. I haven't seen him in a few months and haven't answered his paper grams either. We weren't exactly on good terms.

"Maybe you could write to him," Safari suggested. Even though you aren't together, he deserves to know.

Luna stood up and started pacing around the room.

What's going to happen to me?

To our baby?

"Are you going to tell anyone?" she whimpered.

"No, I won't," Safari reassured. But your belly is only going to get bigger, and people will find out sooner or later. So you need to tell them. It will be a lot worse if they find out on their own. Your mom and Beatrice will be upset but will forgive you over time.

"The real danger lies with the authorities, but Alan might be able to protect you, Safari rationalized." So he needs to know first.

"Okay, you're right," Luna agreed, grabbing some brown parchment from the kitchen. She carefully crafted the note and handed it to Safari to read over.

"Looks good," Safari noted and sealed it in an envelope. Luna prayed that she was doing the right thing.

***

Mr. Smith took another bite of his breakfast omelet, relishing the peaceful morning. His wife sat next to him, sipping coffee, and was reading the *Star City Post*, the local newspaper. His watch chimed, notifying him that StarMart stock had dropped 5 points. He tapped the watch to sell his shares and enjoyed his breakfast. A goddard approached them, holding a brown letter.

"A paper gram for Mr. Alan Smith," the robot beeped. Mrs. Smith studied the mysterious brown letter and dropped it on the plate in disgust.

"It's from floor 3," she recoiled. Mr. Smith was troubled. Why would his son get a message from the ocean floors? He would have to ask him about it later.

"Isn't Alan supposed to have all his mail sent to your sister's condo?" Mrs. Smith noted, eyeing the letter with suspicion.

"Yes, but the post office makes mistakes sometimes," Mr. Smith sniffed and took a bite from his sausage. Mrs. Smith picked the paper gram up and ripped it open.

Erm, darling. Shouldn't we let Alan open that? "He is an adult, and that is his personal business," Mr. Smith warned, something about the letter didn't sit right him.

His business is my business.

"I am his mother, after all," Mrs. Smith huffed and began reading the letter.

"Jen," Mr. Smith forewarned.

He always disliked his wife snooping and prying in their family affairs.

Mrs. Smith started to hyperventilate and screamed at the top of her lungs as if a pack of wolves was attacking her. Mr. Smith shot up and tried to calm his wife. His wife dropped the letter and continued to shriek at the top of her lungs. Her eyes were wild, and she started trembling. She dashed out of the room and slammed the front door. Mr. Smith wanted to follow his wife, but the letter captivated him. He apprehensively picked up the tattered paper off the floor and read it. He gripped his chest and crumpled up the paper in fury. He was used to Logan causing scandal, but Alan... Alan was his good son. He was quiet and always did what he was asked.

He felt shocked, disgusted, and dismayed. He wanted to rip up and burn up the paper. However, he had to confront Alan about this delicate situation and calm his hysterical wife. Both were difficult tasks, and he hoped to enjoy his day off. Mr. Smith activated his watch and sent a video call to his sister. Debbie's bloated face appeared on the screen. She was holding a glass of wine.

"Good morning, Davieeeee," she hiccuped and held up her glass.

"Where's Alan?" Mr. Smith grunted.

"At school," Debbie replied.

Why do you ask?

I need to show you something important.

"I'll be there in an hour," he commanded, ending the video call. It was going to take all his strength not to harm his son.

***

Luna was sprawled out on the couch, reading a mystery novel. Her mother trudged into the room. Bruises were spread along her arms and her cracked lip seeped blood. Luna closed her book and sat upright.

Mum, are you alright?

Her mother poured a glass of whisky and tilted her head back to let the amber liquid flow down her throat.

"Nasty date," she grumbled.

The trick tried to steal my money, but I wasn't having it.

We got into a bit of a disagreement.

Here, put this in the savings jar. Her mother pulled out a wad of hundred bills from the cleavage of her red dress and placed the money in Luna's outstretched

195

hands. Luna pulled out an old coffee container at the bottom of the sink and added the bills to the pile of cash. She looked up at her mother. Dark circles hung around her brown eyes, and her black curls were tangled. As a child, Luna always thought her mother looked glamorous with her short dresses, red lipstick, and black heels. Her mother now looked tired. The years of working the streets she has had taken its toll. It saddened Luna, but she knew her mother could never retire from that line of work.

Her mother lit a cigarette while Luna returned to the couch. Luna's neck prickled as her mother watched her.

You've been wearing a lot of sweatshirts lately. "Are you feeling alright?" her mother inquired while letting smoke roll out of her nose. Luna felt tempted to tell her mother about the baby when a knock at the door interrupted them. Her mother checked the clock in the kitchen.

Hmm, that's weird. "Fred isn't supposed to be here till 7," her mother said and opened the door.

A lovely woman with brown hair and a white dress stood in the doorway. Mascara stained the sides of her cheeks, and she was violently shaking. Luna's stomach dropped. The woman resembled Alan. Luna checked the right side of her chest and saw 378 embroidered in gold.

"Can I help you?" her mother inquired in alarm. The woman paused and shot daggers at Luna. Luna held her breath.

"No, god, not like this," Luna thought.

She stood frozen and watched the chaos unfold.

"That whore, sent me a letter saying that she was pregnant with my son's child," she shrieked at the top of her lungs while pointing at Luna. Rage-filled tears streamed down the woman's face. Her mother gasped.

There must be a mistake, ma'am. What makes you think that?

"I got a paper gram from this address saying that a woman here is pregnant with my son's child, and I demand an explanation," the woman cried.

Her mother recovered from her shock and softened her face.

"Of course, ma'am, Luna, please clarify the situation," her mother said in a cheerful tone. Her mother gave her a look that communicated, *Lie, you stupid bitch.* Luna trembled and pressed her lips together. She decided to start with an apology.

I'm sorry to bother you with the letter, ma'am.

You see, I…I made a mistake and wrote down the wrong tube number. It was supposed to go to floor 14.

"I'm sorry to have distressed you and your family," Luna said, dropping her gaze to the floor. She prayed that his mother would believe the explanation.

"I see," the woman said with a perplexed expression. "That still doesn't explain why it's addressed to Alan," she continued.

The child's father's name is Allanakah," Luna's mother interjected. We call him Alan for short. "Again, I am incredibly sorry that my daughter's stupidity has disturbed you and your family," she replied, glaring at Luna.

Luna said nothing and placed her hands in her pockets to keep them from trembling. Relief spread across the woman's face, and she wiped away her tears.

Thank you for clarifying. I didn't mean to barge in here like I did. I just couldn't stomach the shame this would cause my family. I guess I overreacted. She let out a hysterical laugh and grinned. I should have trusted my Alan. "He's such a good boy," the woman said.

"I'm sure he is," Luna's mother agreed. There is nothing wrong with being a caring mother. Is there anything else you need from us?

"No," the woman sniffled. Thank you. Take care. The woman departed, and her mother closed the door.

Luna felt a wave of terror as her mother turned towards her. Her fists were clenched, and she was glowering over her. "Unzip your sweatshirt, now," she ordered. Luna obeyed and exposed her swelling stomach. Her mother gasped in horror and turned away.

"When were you going to tell me?" she rasped and crossed her arms.

Soon, I just didn't know how. "I'm sorry you had to find out like this," Luna whimpered.

"So, it's true," her mother said, her voice rippling in pain.

"Yes," Luna trembled. Her mother descended on her and seized her arm. She yanked Luna up and started pelting her with her left hand.

How could you?

How could you lie with them after what they did to Darnelle?

After what they do to our family, your friends?

How could you betray us?

"Have I taught you nothing," her mother screeched while slapping her. Luna held her arm up to shield herself from her mother's blows.

"I'm sorry, mother," Luna wept. I'm sorry.

Her mother stopped and let go of her arm. Her face contorted with rage and pain. "I want you out," her mother commanded.

"Mum, I don't have anywhere to go," Luna whimpered.

"You should've thought of that before bringing home a baby in your belly," her mother snapped. You want to make adult decisions. You will be treated like an adult. So, it's time to move out.

Luna wanted to cry, to beg for her mother's forgiveness, but she knew from her mother's expression that she had made up her mind. Luna collected a few clothes, her journal, and a sock full of money and shoved it into her work bag. Her mother sat at the kitchen table lost in thought. Luna stood in front of the table. This was probably the last time she would ever see her.

"Goodbye, Mum," she said sadly. Her mother didn't respond. She walked towards the door. A picture of Darnelle hung next to it. *Would he have kicked her out or defended her?* Luna reflected. *It doesn't matter, he's dead,* she thought bitterly. Luna gingerly placed her hand on the frame and wished him goodbye.

***

Alan tossed his accounting notes and textbooks on the sofa. He stretched, relieved to be out of his classes.

"Goddard, can you get me a glass of water?" he announced. The yellow robot whizzed up, carrying a glass of water, and handed it to him.

"Your aunt, Logan, and father are waiting for you in the dining room," it beeped. Alan's father rarely visited him. He was usually traveling or busy at the office. *It must be important,* Alan thought. Alan sipped his water and walked into the dining room. All three of his family members were sitting at the table. Aunt Debbie and his father wore somber expressions while his brother sat with his arms crossed and looked smug.

"Where's mom?" Alan asked, scanning the room.

"Have a seat, son," his father ordered, motioning towards the chair across from him.

Alan sat down, apprehension, making his hands prickle. He felt like he was at an intervention, except he was in the hot seat instead of Logan.

"We received some distressing news this morning that has sent your mother into one of her episodes," he explained. We want to handle this with the utmost care, but I need you to verify if the information disclosed in this message is true. His father handed him a brown paper. Alan recognized the parchment from Luna. His heart sank, and he read the contents of the paper.

Dear Alan, I want first to say I'm sorry for not answering your previous messages, but things have not been great for my friend Beatrice. She is in trouble, and we have worked tirelessly to help her. Anyway, I am reaching out because I have some important news that you need to know. I'm pregnant with your child. I'm not expecting you to respond or see me because things have been rocky. But I wanted you to know. I'll update you when I find out if it's a boy or a girl. I love you. Let me know when you finish school.

-Luna

Alan blinked and placed the paper on the table. He was trying his hardest not to vomit from nerves.

"Please tell me mom didn't read this," he said shakily.

"She was the first to read it, and it about killed her," his father replied. Alan closed his eyes and rubbed his face. This was the very last thing he wanted her to know.

"So again, we need to know if this is true," his dad pressed, his expression serious. Alan looked over at his brother. A smirk curled on his lips. He was entertained by Alan's misery. He studied Aunt Debbie. She was eerily sober and wore a tight-lipped appearance. Alan was tempted to lie, to deny the situation, but he couldn't bring himself to it.

"Yes, it's true, but this is my first time hearing this," Alan admitted. His father slammed his fist on the table in a fury.

How could you bring this shame on our family? "She's an undesirable, a bottom feeder," he spat.

Alan flinched and looked away.

His Aunt gripped his wrist.

Dave, we talked about this. "No sense in fussing over spilled milk," she soothed.

It's disgusting and unnatural. "And I do not like this," his father boomed, pointing at the letter.

Alan wanted to escape the room, but he remained seated.

I know you are upset, Dave. "I'm ashamed of it myself," Aunt Debbie continued, eyeing Alan disdainfully. But we need to find Jen, and Alan may be the only one that can help.

The front door burst open, interrupting their heated argument. Alan's mother walked in. She looked like a mad woman that crawled out of the swamp. Her face was ruddy, and her hair was matted with sweat and ash. Her clothing and boots were caked in mud. Her eyes darted wildly around the room.

"My Alan, my sweet Alan," she wailed and rushed towards him. Alan braced himself to be struck but was surprised to be covered in sloppy kisses. The other family members exchanged looks of confusion.

"Mom, what happened to you?" Logan inquired.

"Oh, I received the most wonderful news," she beamed. It was a mistake, you see. I went to the location that was posted on the paper gram and confronted the person who accused my son of such a horrific deed. She informed me that she had sent the letter to the wrong address and the father's name was Alli- something. It was some foreign name. "Anyway, all that matters is it's not you, my dear," she exclaimed to Alan and hugged him.

Alan lightly patted his mother's back. He imagined his mother crashing into the cramped apartment. *Poor Luna,* he thought to himself.

"Glad it worked out, Mom," Alan said. You should get cleaned up and some rest.

"Yes, that's a wonderful idea," his father vocalized, leading his mother towards the door. "Thank you, Debbie, for having us over," he smiled.

"Pleasure," Debbie hummed. "Oh, it was horrible, Dave," his mother prattled on. They live in such squalor with bugs everywhere. I'll have to burn my clothes.

"Yes, my dear," his father mumbled, closing the door behind them.

Logan smacked Alan on the back.

"Congratulations on being a father!" he said sarcastically.

"Logan, this is not the time," Aunt Debbie snapped. I would like a word alone with your brother.

Logan's smile faded.

"Hey, goddard, set up my gaming set," Logan ordered the robot and walked into the living room.

"Alan, what you have done is disgraceful," she seethed. And I am disappointed and ashamed of you.

Alan lowered his eyes to the granite table. His Aunt's words cut deeper than his father's angry shouts.

How could you do that to her?

"I didn't know," Alan protested. I found out at the same time as you did. Alan motioned to the letter.

"You know what I mean," his aunt growled.

Alan was lost for words.

Alan, do you know why your parents discourage you from being with people in lower sectors?

"Because it's indecent," Alan repeated the mantra he had heard so many times from his mother.

Yes, but it is also illegal, and you've indirectly put her life in danger. You think you love this girl but you are just young and confused.

"I'm not confused," Alan retorted, anger boiled in his chest.

"These feelings will pass as you age, and you'll find someone more suitable," his aunt continued.

I don't want to be with anyone else. I want to be there for her and our kid. "Is that such a horrible thing?" Alan protested.

"No, you will make their life harder," Aunt Debbie explained.

There are forces in place to keep our world balanced, and when you go against them, it only leads to ruin. Alan understood what she meant. He thought of Luna's injured eye and the authorities that Beatrice complained about. Aunt Debbie reached for Alan's hand and held it.

Alan, if you care for this girl, you'll keep your distance.

"That means no messages and no visits while you are under my roof," she demanded.

Are we at an understanding?

Alan agreed, and Aunt Debbie went to refill her empty wine glass. Alan made a silent promise to provide for Luna and his unborn child a better life. He retrieved the textbooks from the couch and started studying.

Chapter 18

GRIEF

"Here's your cut," Luna said, handing Delta a stack of bills. Delta handed over Luna's son and counted the money.

"How is my Oliver?" Luna cooed and gently swayed back and forth. Her son's hazel eyes glinted with delight, and he laughed. Luna flattened down tiny tufts of black hair and kissed his forehead.

"Thank you for watching him," Luna said to Delta.

"No worries, my dear," Delta replied, fanning herself. At least you work. "Unlike some of my other children," she spat at a bundle of hackneyed blankets at her feet. Gina poked her head out from underneath the blankets. She sucked in her teeth and pulled the blanket over her head. Delta scowled. Luna sat on a green couch in the living room.

Delta placed the money in her robes and joined her. Luna felt relieved to sit down after a long day at the Tilapia plant and hold her precious son. She felt guilty not being able to raise him all hours of the day, but she needed the money. That was part of her agreement with Delta, so she had to continue to work.

Luna was thankful that Delta took her in, even though quarters were packed.

"Where's your sister?" Delta demanded while adjusting her head wrap.

I think Safari went to see Hugo about new costume designs. "She'll be home soon," Luna reassured.

Well, I hope she comes back soon. We have a competition tonight, and a lot of work must be done. "Go ahead and wake up the others and start dinner," Delta ordered. "I'll be making myself beautiful," she broadcasted and drifted to her bedroom.

Luna placed Oliver on the couch and wrapped a blanket around him to ensure he would stay in place.

"Be good," she whispered to him. Oliver kicked his feet and smiled. Luna attempted to rouse the house members who were fast asleep in the middle of the living room floor. Waking them was often difficult due to them staying up all hours of the night. Luna was about to give up when Oliver started crying.

"Oh no, Oliver," Luna cried, rushing back to the couch. She rocked him slowly and shushed him.

"Ugh, does that baby ever sleep," one of the members groaned and pushed the blankets to the side.

"Sorry, Damien, he's just feeling a bit fussy right now," Luna apologized and tried to coax her baby into silence. Damien was short, a muscular man with tan skin and cornrows.

"I'd be fussy too if I had to see that face every day," a heavy-set Latino man teased next to him.

"You're not funny, Fernando," Damien groaned and closed his eyes.

"I think it's just nature's alarm clock," another member yawned and sat up. I'll get them moving if you want to start dinner.

"Thanks, Harley," Luna responded, bringing Oliver into the kitchen. Harley pushed his warped mohawk back in place and started shaking the other members.

Luna placed Oliver in a cloth carrier and pulled out a metal pot covered in dents. She turned on the faucet and let the rusty water empty. When the water turned from brown to clear, she filled the pot with water and placed it on one of the black burners. She had trouble lighting the propane stove, so she manually activated it with a match. Oliver clapped at the blue flames in delight. Luna wiped down the counters and pulled cheap ceramic bowls from the cupboards. The water began to boil, and she added two boxes of noodles.

"Spaghetti again," Damien complained from the doorway.

" It's the best way to feed a family of seven," Luna remarked, stirring the noodles with a wooden spoon. Maybe I can pick up something different when I go grocery shopping tomorrow. What do you want?

"Pizza," Fernando interjected.

"Mother would never allow it. We have to watch our figures, remember," Damien snapped.

"I know that's why I need a pizza, to help my figure get curvier," Fernando replied and struck a seductive pose.

"Aren't you all supposed to be getting ready?" Safari interrupted and put her hands on her hips.

"Can't, Gina's hogging the bathroom again," Damien sighed.

"Well, if you aren't going to get ready, you can help me with dinner," Luna suggested as she chopped onions.

"On second thought, we can rehearse our number while we wait," Fernando said, and both men disappeared from the doorway.

"How's my Oliver?" Safari exclaimed with outstretched arms. Oliver let out a shriek of delight and waved his arms. Luna pulled him out of the carrier and passed him to Safari. Safari spun her son around as Luna tossed the onions into a cast iron with oil.

"He's so adorable," Safari continued. He's got your facial features. He could be your twin. Except for

"Except for his eyes," Luna interrupted and dumped a jar of tomato sauce in the pan.

"He's got his dad's eyes," she echoed, sorrow lingering in her voice. Safari pressed her lips together.

"Has he responded yet?" she asked tentatively.

"No, but I'm sure he has his reasons," Luna sighed and stirred the contents of the pot. And I'm kind of okay with it. After his mother crashed into our apartment. I'm sure she banned him from ever talking to me again.

"Still, it's his loss," Safari said, carrying Oliver into the living room.

Luna sat in silence for a moment. She wanted to be mad at Alan for not being there for them, but a part of her missed him. She added spaghetti noodles and sauce to the glass bowls.

"Dinner's ready," she announced to the living room and started washing dishes. Gina and Harley gathered their bowls first, their faces covered in gothic makeup. Fernando and Damien came in next, breathing heavily and covered in perspiration. Safari was the last one and brought back a cheerful Oliver.

"I'll take care of Mother," Safari informed her, and Luna handed her two bowls.

Luna placed her bowl on the wooden kitchen table and nursed Oliver. She took a few bites of her meal and patted Oliver on his back to help him burp. Luna finished her meal as Oliver slipped into a peaceful slumber. The house members were dressed in gold robes and were excitedly chatting about the competition. They dropped dirty dishes in the sink and went to practice their dance routines in the living room. Luna missed that part of her life.

Since she became a mother, her life has become dull. She went to work at the factory and then came home to clean and take care of Oliver. All of her money went to Oliver and Delta, so she had to give up her dream of saving up to live near the Deep-Sea Aquarium. She wondered if this was how her mother felt when she was all alone with her and Darnelle.

Luna reminded herself that she was in a better situation than her mother and should be thankful.

Luna looked down at Oliver and was filled with peace. The love she felt for him made all the hardship and strife worth it. A loud bang reverberated through the apartment as the front door broke off its hinges. Luna screamed and clutched her baby to her chest. A stream of hooded men with pink triangles on their chests, carrying guns, stormed the kitchen. Luna sank to the ground, shielding her son. Oliver let out cries of protest. Delta ran into the kitchen and threw her hands up as the men pointed their guns at her.

"What is the meaning of this?" she boomed in fury. The men parted as a man with a pink jumpsuit and feathers around his cuffs and neck stood in front of Delta. His cowboy boots and hat sparkled in the fluorescent light. He watched Delta behind star-shaped shades.

"Delta, you look beautiful today. I take it you're going to another ball," Hoodi grinned.

"Get out of my home," she shrieked, blocking the door.

"Well, that's no polite way to greet your guest," Hoodi replied, pulling out his gun. He aimed it at Delta. Delta breathed hard.

"What do you want?" she shouted and stepped back. "You don't know," he drawled. I'm just doing business. They all stood frozen in silence. Luna wanted to throw something at him or charge out the door, but she didn't dare move. Delta attempted to run into the living room, and Hoodi fired his gun. The bullet hit the back of Delta's neck, causing her head to lurch backward.

Brain matter, blood, and hair sprayed all over the floor as Delta collapsed. Luna let out a shriek in terror and curled up into a ball. Oliver's muffled cries filled her chest. The members of the house cried and screamed in horror at their dead mother.

"Seize them," Hoodi ordered, and the henchmen descended on her family. Harley flung himself at Hoodi and landed a powerful punch on Hoodi's jaw. Hoodi lurched his head back in pain and fired at Harley. A bullet ricocheted through Harley's throat. Harley grabbed his throat as blood gushed out of it. He let out horrible gurgling sounds before dying on the floor. Hoodi's henchmen tightened zip ties around the other members' hands and shoved dirty rags into their mouths to stifle their screams. Hoodi watched in silent satisfaction as they struggled against the henchman— one by one, they were draped out of the apartment.

Hoodi cracked his neck and approached Luna. Tears streamed down her face, and she clutched Oliver tighter. His little cries grew louder. Hoodi lowered himself and pointed the gun towards the floor.

Please.

"Please don't kill him," Luna wept and shook her head.

"Jesus Christ, I'm not a monster," Hoodi replied.

Now, let's see the little guy. He put his gun in his pocket and held out his arms. Luna shook her head and pressed her back against the wall.

No.

"No, I won't let you take him," Luna protested. Hoodi returned his hand to his gun when a ringtone resounded from his pocket.

He muttered to himself in annoyance and stood up. He pulled out a pink rhinestone-encrusted flip phone and answered. He listened as the other person squawked on the other end of the call.

Hello. Okay. Okay. Ricky, can't this wait? "I'm a bit busy," he told the person. *Okay. Okay. "Bye honey,"* Hoodi said affectionately and blew a kiss into the phone.

"Sorry about that," he apologized and put the phone away. "It looks like today is your lucky day," he announced dismissively and stepped over Delta's dead body.

"Duty calls," he waved and departed. The rest of the henchmen followed and disappeared into the night.

Luna whimpered at Delta's corpse. Her eyes stared vacantly at her, and her wig fell off, exposing her short hair underneath a hair net. A pool of viscous blood surrounded her. Oliver was wailing at the top of his lungs. His face was ruddy from crying. Luna hummed, trying to calm him and take her mind off the horrific scene she witnessed. Her legs felt like jelly, but she knew she had to move.

Oliver stopped crying, and Luna summoned the courage to move. Luna fled the scene and ran her hands along the wooded panels of the hallway. She shuffled across the old moldy carpet and banged on the metal doors. She cried out for help. Praying for someone, anyone would let her in. No one responded. They were probably too afraid of getting killed themselves to answer.

Luna sank to the floor. Her mind was racing. She couldn't go to the police. They never went below floor four at night. Her mother disowned her, and Beatrice was in prison. She felt so lost and alone. She sat on the carpet and rocked Oliver until he fell asleep. Vivid memories of her friends being taken and Delta dying replayed in her mind. Luna tried to shut them out and think of happier times. Good times with Safari, Darnelle, and Alan.

The door across from her creaked open, and Mrs. Ang's withered face appeared in the darkness. Her eyes darted around the hallway, and then she motioned for Luna to come in. Luna obeyed and entered a dark room that smelled of incense and herbs. Mrs. Ang lit a few candles on a plain table and signaled for Luna to sit on a red cushion.

"Place baby here," she whispered, pointing to another cushion on the right side of Luna. Luna tenderly put Oliver on the cushion and covered him with the baby blanket Damien made for him. His chest rose and fell as he slept. Mrs. Ang skittered into the kitchen while Luna scanned the dimly lit room. The room was immaculate and adorned with Chinese art. Luna admired the nicely decorated room even though the walls were stained with soot and the carpet stank of mildew.

Mrs. Ang appeared with a teapot and a tray with ornate cups. She placed the cup before Luna and poured hot tea into it.

"Drink, it will calm your nerves," Mrs. Ang instructed and pressed her thin lips together. Luna admired the elegant blue crane painted on the cup and drank the tea. The scent of chamomile and lavender brought back fond memories of Darnelle and the tea parties he would host when they were kids.

"Thank you," Luna said, holding the tea in her lap.

"What happened there?" Mrs. Ang inquired while savoring her tea. It sounds like someone was getting murdered. Luna explained what happened while wiping away her tears. Mrs. Ang listened intently and nodded sympathetically. She handed Luna a handkerchief when she concluded her story.

You are not safe on this floor. You need to find somewhere else to stay. "He will come back and finish the job," Mrs. Ang warned. I want to help, but I cannot hide you.

Think hard.

What are your options?

Luna explained her situation with her mother and Beatrice.

"What about baby's father?" Mrs. Ang suggested and motioned towards Oliver.

"He lives far away, and I'm unsure if he could help me," Luna replied.

How far? "What floor?" Mrs. Ang pressed. It's in the Star Sector, floor 152, I think. Mrs. Ang raised her eyebrows in surprise.

"That is far," she admitted. But safe, so you have to try. Mrs. Ang stood, then handed Luna a pen and paper. "Ask him to meet you where sparkly man won't find you," Mrs. Ang suggested.

Luna thought hard. It would have to be somewhere Alan was familiar with, and it had to be in the Ocean Sector because she didn't have clearance past floor 50. The Ballroom and the Aquarium were too crowded, so that wouldn't work.

Her mind drifted to her time with Alan. Fond memories of star gazing, overlooking the city lights, and their first kiss. *The Angelfish courtyard!* Luna thought. That would be the perfect place. Luna held her breath as she wrote a message on the thin paper. Mrs. Ang rummaged through a wooden desk and pulled out an envelope. Luna carefully placed the letter in and sealed it.

"It's time to rest," Mrs. Ang advised, laying down a blanket and a pillow in the corner of the living room. Luna brought the cushion and Oliver next to her. Don't worry. We will take care of your friends tomorrow morning. "Authorities lazy and only come down during bankers' hours," Mrs. Ang snarled in disgust. Make sure you deliver letter, and don't give up. Luna thanked her and tenderly stroked Oliver's hair. Mrs. Ang blew out the candles, sending her into darkness. Luna silently sobbed into the pillow, mourning her beloved friends and praying things would get better.

Chapter 19

AFFLUENT

Alan dropped the last box of clothes in the empty bedroom and sat on the floor.

"Are we done moving all your crap yet?" Logan complained.

"Yes," Alan responded, wiping the sweat off his forehead.

"Alright, time for a beer break," Logan announced and handed Alan a can of Starlite. Alan placed the cool can on his forehead while Logan chugged his. Alan was relieved to finally be able to move into his apartment. Even though he still had to unpack all his belongings, he was happy to have his own space and not have to deal with his aunt's drunk shenanigans.

"So, are you going to throw a house party?" Logan asked.

"No, I have school and work tomorrow," Alan replied.

"Lame," Logan jeered and cracked open another beer. How's balancing checkbooks for old ladies?

"It sucks, but it pays enough for me to rent this place," Alan replied.

Yeah, but on floor 150, the view here sucks.

"Hey, beggars can't be choosers," Alan shrugged. Don't you have some awesome party to go to?

Nah, I gotta be on my best behavior for a bit. "Dad said if I failed my drug test again, he would send me to rehab," Logan explained.

"Wow, your life is so hard," Alan mocked.

"Shut up, loser," Logan shouted and punched him in the shoulder. Alan held his shoulder in pain and chuckled. He always enjoyed annoying his brother.

"So, are you still talking to that ocean girl you knocked up?" Logan smirked.

"No, I didn't want to upset the family any more than I already had," Alan admitted. I still feel bad about not being there.

"Don't beat yourself up, bro. Lots of businessmen have bastards from lower sectors," Logan said. It's just how things are.

"That does not make me feel better," Alan replied. I'm going to start unpacking boxes. Would you check the mail room and make sure there are none left? "I think mom sent me some of her old china," Alan continued, trying to change the subject.

"Uggh, fine," Logan whined and made his way towards the door. I guess I'll just keep working like a servant and carry up all these heavy packages by myself.

Alan rolled his eyes and began placing his books on the shelf. His astronomy textbook on the Kuiper belt fell, and Luna's paper grams spilled all over the floor. Many of them were from the earlier part of their friendship and mostly contained clippings of marine animals. Alan knew he should probably throw them away, but he couldn't completely erase her from his life. He placed them back in the textbook and added books to the shelf.

"Hey Alan," Logan announced from behind him. Logan wore a solemn expression and held a brown envelope. "I think you might want to read this," he said.

"You opened it," Alan grumbled in irritation.

"Of course, how else would I blackmail you and become the favorite sibling," Logan joked. Anyway, you need to read it.

Alan pulled out the letter.

Dear Alan, I know we haven't spoken in a while, and I understand why, with your family and everything. But I need your help. I am reaching out to you because Oliver and I are in danger. I can't say too much in this message, just in case it gets intercepted. You know who attacked us last night, and I need to leave the 2nd floor. I know you may not care for me anymore, but please do this for our son if you can. Meet me at the Angelfish Fountain at 8 pm. I love you.

-Luna

"So, are you gonna go?" Logan pressed after Alan finished reading the message.

Perhaps. "Are you gonna tell on me?" Alan asked.

Not at the moment. "But if you go missing, I might change my mind," Logan replied. The brothers sat in silence for a moment.

"Thanks," Alan said timidly and added clothes to his closet.

"Welp, if you don't need help anymore," Logan yawned. I'm going to go smoke and go hang with Cody. "Smell you later, loser," Logan deflected and gave Alan a hard shove before leaving. Alan sighed and looked over the letter. He was silently hoping that he would be able to rescue Luna.

***

Luna sat on the stone bench and watched Oliver sleep. The day had been an emotionally draining one. That morning, she had to make a police report on Delta and Harley's murders. She couldn't bring herself to go in the room, so she made the statement in the hallway. The officer promised they would investigate it, but it was unlikely due to Hoodi's influence over the city. She had heard whispers of him doing the same thing around different parts of the sector. Many believed he had either blackmailed the Ocean Sector authorities or was bribing them to look the other way. Luna wanted revenge, to make him suffer, but it still wouldn't bring her friends back. She also contemplated what happened to Safari and the other members of the house. Had they been sold? Killed? Or they might be working for him now? All in all, she felt powerless and utterly alone.

Alan appeared at the center of the archway carrying a small backpack. His appearance was haggard, but he was still handsome. Luna stood up and smiled. She wanted to rush over to embrace him, but she wasn't entirely sure if he still had feelings for her. So, she stayed in place. Alan steadily approached her and looked down at the bundle in her arms.

"Is this him?" he asked avidly.

Luna nodded.

Would you like to hold him?

"Please," Alan breathed and held out his arms. Luna delicately placed Oliver into Alan's hands. Alan cradled him, and Oliver awoke from his slumber. Oliver gurgled and beamed at him.

"He likes you," Luna commented. He usually cries when he meets strangers.

"He's so small," Alan gasped as Oliver clutched his finger. How old is he?

"Only five months, he still has much growing to do," Luna sighed.

I'm sorry I wasn't there for you or him. "My family threatened to kick me out if I continued to contact you," Alan explained.

I thought so.

"Your mom was really scary when I met her," Luna replied.

"Yeah, she gets so crazy when she feels our reputation is threatened," Alan affirmed. One time, she had a meltdown because the host didn't like the spiced

222

wine we brought to a dinner party. Aww, it sounds like she's so hard on herself. "It has to be tiresome, worrying about what others think all the time," Luna continued. I think if I were like that, I'd be crazy too.

"So, what did you need to tell me?" Alan inquired.

I need a place to stay. Hoodi killed and kidnapped the family that I was living with. My mother disowned me when she found out I was pregnant with Oliver, and Beatrice is in prison. I've been living with our neighbor, Mrs. Ang, for a bit, but she thinks that Hoodi might attack again. So, she suggested I try to hide on the higher floors for a bit. I know I'm asking a lot of you. "But I just need a place to stay until things calm down, or I can save up for a place to live," Luna explained.

Alan hesitated, and Luna anxiously waited for a response.

"You can stay with me for a while," Alan suggested.

"Wouldn't your family take issue with that?" Luna questioned and furrowed her brow.

I've distanced myself from them and moved out. "I was planning on sending you money to support Oliver when I finished school," Alan said.

Are you sure? "I don't want you to get in trouble with the law," Luna expressed.

Alan shrugged.

They will just give me a fine. I've seen my aunt wiggle out of some sticky situations with the law, and I'll be discreet this go around. The trick is a good lawyer. *That's what Beatrice needs*, Luna thought to herself.

"Thank you, Alan," Luna said and embraced him. Alan pulled her in closer and planted a soft kiss on her lips. Oliver cooed, and they both looked down at him affectionately.

"So, I need you to put this on," Alan murmured, handing Luna a white dress. It will help you blend in better. Luna pulled off the blue tunic Safari had let her borrow and slipped on the gown. Alan shoved the tunic into the bag.

"We can switch out your boots when we get to the Cloud Sector rest stop," Alan continued.

"You really thought of everything," Luna commented.

Logan gave me some interesting tips. "Apparently, some of his friends woudl occasionally sneak ocean hookers in for parties," Alan stated.

Luna blinked, this didn't surprise her.

"Ready to go?" Alan asked.

Yes.

Luna held Oliver and followed Alan into the night.

Luna washed her face and hair with the soap in the restroom just as Alan instructed her. She felt guilty as she left a ring of dirt around the sink and cleaned it as best as she could with paper towels. She braided her hair and put on the new white boots that Alan pulled out of his bag. Luna prayed that his plan would work. She carried her black tennis shoes out of the bathroom and handed them to Alan. Alan was sitting in the waiting area, cradling Oliver, who was fast asleep. So, here comes the tricky part.

"We have to get Oliver past the welcome desk," Alan explained. And you won't like it, but you have to trust me.

Luna swallowed hard and nodded.

Logan strolled into the room carrying a picnic basket in one hand and a beer in the other.

"Is that my nephew?" Logan slurred and waddled over to get a better look at the sleeping baby.

"If you wake him up, I will kill you," Alan threatened.

"You're welcome," Logan sneered and handed the picnic basket to Luna.

"What's important is we go slow and quietly to ensure that we don't wake the baby," Alan continued, placing Oliver in the basket. Luna hesitated.

"What if he wakes up and starts crying?" she inquired.

"Easy, you run back into the elevator and go back to where you came from," Logan quipped.

"Don't worry, he won't," Alan reassured. Just let Logan and I do the talking.

Luna didn't like the plan but was determined to try.

"Okay, but I'm carrying him," Luna demanded.

Luna closed the lid to the picnic basket, and they boarded the elevator. Alan scanned his key card and typed in a code into the keypad.

"Uggh, that makes it so much longer," Logan complained. Alan shushed him.

"We are doing it to keep the baby asleep," he mouthed. Logan grumbled, and they steadily ascended upwards. Luna followed Alan and Logan to the front desk, where they held the basket. Logan handed the key card to the desk attendant and winked at her.

"Your new tits look pretty great, Jen," Logan broadcasted.

"Wow, how romantic?" Luna thought to herself and resisted the urge to roll her eyes. The woman giggled while the blond attendant next to her wore a jealous expression.

"Thanks, I just got them done," the brunette attendant shared.

"Are you going to Deb's party tonight?" the other attendant interrupted, trying to catch Logan's attention.

"Perhaps," Logan replied nonchalantly. Depends on who's there.

"What's she doing here?" the brunette attendant sneered and pointed at Luna.

"Oh, she's bringing party favors," Logan proclaimed. Do you want a sample? Both women looked at each other and grinned.

"Well, you got to keep this between us, if you know what I mean," Logan whispered and winked.

The women giggled again. Logan slipped them a baggie with purple dust in it. The women stuck their pinkies in the bag and scooped some powder with their white nails. They sniffed it and perked up.

"That's good," the brunette commented, placing the baggie in her pocket.

"Can I see her key card?" the blond attendant motioned. Luna handed her key card to Alan. The woman shoved it into a machine and returned her key card and a Day Pass.

"So, she should be good for a week," the brunette attendant informed them. But try not to go past floor 153 or any other sectors.

"Thank you," Alan stated.

"Thank you," Logan boomed, and the women erupted into giggles. Logan winked and led them away from the welcome desk into a glass tube with a concrete floor connected the city. Luna tried not to look to the sides or downward and focused on the back of Alan's head. That went way better than she expected.

"How do they know you?" Alan demanded.

"Oh, I banged both of them at Chris's Halloween party, and let's just say they couldn't resist my smokin' hot body," Logan declared and flexed his muscles.

"Wow, you're so humble and modest," Alan sneered sarcastically.

Exactly! "That's why everyone loves me," Logan boasted, oblivious to his brother's snide remarks.

"Thank you for helping us get in," Luna interjected.

Oh, don't thank me yet. "Alan owes me big time," Logan spouted and ruffled Alan's hair. Alan muttered to himself and brushed his hair down.

They came to a halt at a gray tower with several rows of small windows. The outside perimeter was embellished with green shrubs and yellow petunias.

"Welp, it's time for me to go," Logan announced. "Try. to wear a condom this time. Mom doesn't need another heart attack," Logan joked and waved goodbye. Luna placed the hand over her mouth to suppress a laugh while Alan turned pink.

"Your brother is so rude but weirdly charismatic," Luna commented as they walked towards Alan's apartment.

"Yeah, I think that's just how he expresses love," Alan replied, unlocking the apartment door. By insulting me non-stop.

Luna placed the picnic basket on the counter and was relieved to finally take out Oliver. Oliver began to cry from the sudden movement. Luna hummed comforting words and hugged him.

"Oliver, you were so good," she sang to him, and the baby was nullified and went back to sleep.

Are the walls thin? I would hate to bother your neighbors.

"Oliver can be fussy when he's not feeling well," Luna noted.

I think we'll be okay. The complex is relatively new and not very luxurious, so I don't have many neighbors at the moment. "I occasionally see a lady walking her dog, but she's at the office a lot," Alan responded.

"It's so empty," Luna observed, scanning the living room.

I just moved in.

I'd be happy to help you unpack. "I don't have to clock in until Monday," Luna offered.

"Please make yourself at home," Alan said. Luna dropped her work bag at the door and pulled off her shoes. She placed Oliver on the couch.

"Do you have a blanket I could wrap him in?" she asked.

"Goddard blanket," Alan commanded, and a robot brought her a red quilt.

"I'll have to get used to that," she shared and wrapped Oliver into a bundle. Exhaustion hit Luna, and she desperately wanted to rest.

Where would you like me to sleep?

"Well, it's only a one-bedroom, so you can have my bed," Alan suggested.

"I can't take your bed from you," Luna sputtered. I'll sleep on the floor with the baby.

What?! You're not sleeping on the floor. You can have my bed. "It's fine," Alan said firmly.

Are you sure-

"Yes," Alan interjected.

If it makes you feel better, I'll sleep in here. Luna didn't have the energy to argue.

"I'm going to head to bed," Luna breathed. Goodnight, and thank you. Luna crawled into the bed and closed her eyes.

***

Alan sat on the living room floor studying his accounting notes. His eyes felt heavy, but his thoughts kept him awake. He looked over at Oliver his son was peacefully sleeping. He felt lucky to meet his son and that they were safe. Alan wondered if the deal he made with Hoodi endangered his family and haunted him. Luna started thrashing and crying in the other room. Alan closed his textbook and went to check on her. She was covered in sweat and muttering to herself. *She's probably having a nightmare,* Alan concluded. I would, too, if my friends were killed in front of me.

"Safari... Damien," she breathed.

No...

Alan sat on the bed, unsure if he should wake her. Luna jolted up and gasped. She pressed her face against his chest and started trembling. He felt tears soak his shirt, and she was breathing hard. Alan drew her in and rubbed her back.

"It's just a dream," he soothed and attempted to comfort her. Luna stopped shaking, and her breathing steadied. She poked her head up and looked around.

Is Oliver alright?

Yeah, he's still on the couch," Alan answered and motioned to the other room.

"Thank god," Luna mumbled into his chest. They sat there for a while, embracing each other. Alan rested his face on her head and listened to her heartbeat.

"Alan, I'm glad you're here," she whispered, facing him. Alan smiled and loosened his grip.

"Do you still love me?" she breathed, searching his face.

"I never stopped," he replied.

Luna pressed forward and kissed him. Alan pulled her in closer and instinctively ran his fingers down her back. He pushed away and shifted his hips to the side in embarrassment. Luna looked down at his pants, and understanding crept across her face. She smiled and kissed him again. Luna slowly lowered her kisses to his chest and then his stomach.

Alan felt warmth spread below his stomach, and he gripped her head. *Is this really happening to me?* he thought and closed his eyes, savoring the moment. He tensed up and let out a gasp of relief. He pressed his head against the bedpost, and Luna lifted her head. She sat up and wiped her mouth.

"Are you alright?" she asked.

"I'm great," he gasped. You didn't have to do that.

"I know, but I wanted to," she shrugged. "I'm not having another baby," she snapped and drifted to the kitchen. Alan rubbed the back of his neck. *I wouldn't mind having that every night,* he thought.

Alan resisted the urge to fall asleep and hopped off the bed. Luna was holding a glass of water and peering out the window.

What's on your mind? "You look pensive," Alan noted.

"I'm thinking about my family, mainly Beatrice," she replied. I'm up here safe, and they're still in trouble down there.

Alan wrapped his arms around her and rested his head on her shoulders.

"How did Beatrice end up in prison?" he inquired.

I think Hoodi framed her the assault report that your brother filed, but we haven't been able to prove it. "Harold says we can fight it if we have a good lawyer, but we can't afford one," Luna responded.

"I might know someone, but we'll save that for tomorrow," Alan yawned and pulled on her hand.

Luna turned and followed him to bed.

***

Oliver's cries woke Luna from a deep sleep. She flung the bed sheets aside and rushed into the living room. Oliver was squirming in his blanket, and his fists were clenched in protest. Luna picked him up and tried her best to soothe him. She nursed him, and his cries died down. Luna fought off grogginess as she continued to comfort him. An alarm went off in Alan's room, and the window that overlooked space was transformed into a screen that looped an animation of flowers underneath

232

a dazzling sun. Alan slumped out of bed and greeted her.

Are you up already?

"Yes, Oliver needed some attention," Luna replied. Alan rubbed his face and stretched. I need to change and get ready for work.

"Feel free to ask Goddard for anything," Alan shared and closed the bedroom door.

Um, goddard," Luna squeaked, looking around the empty room. A miniature robot rolled out from a panel in the wall and stood in front of Luna. It was yellow and had two lenses for eyes.

"What can I do for you, Miss?" the robot buzzed. Luna found the tiny robot to be cute and felt at ease.

"Can you make breakfast and two cups of coffee?" Luna asked timidly, not sure what to expect.

Certainly!

Please select your breakfast and drink options. The robot held out a tablet displaying an assortment of breakfast items. Luna scrolled through the list of items with her finger. She was overwhelmed by the variety of food displayed. Luna didn't recognize a lot of the items. She panicked and clicked the first option.

"You selected southwest breakfast omelet," goddard beeped. Please press submit to place your order. Luna pushed the green button on the tablet. Another goddard came out of the wall in the kitchen. It pulled out ingredients from the refrigerator and started chopping several vegetables. Its hands changed into different utensils as it prepared the meal. Luna gawked in fascination.

"Your coffee, Miss," the goddard chimed and held up the tablet. The screen changed and showed 200 options for coffee. Luna clicked the first option, and the robot pulled out two ceramic mugs full of steaming hot coffee from its chest cavity. Luna took the coffee cups and placed them on the glass table.

"Oh, don't forget coasters," the robot beeped and put them underneath the coffee.

Anything else?

"A change of clothes for Oliver and I would be wonderful," she told the robot.

Will do!

The robot rushed out of the room while the robot that prepared their meal strutted in. The robot was humanoid in shape and carried the plates to the table. It wore a chef's hat and apron.

"Your omelet," it broadcasted and set the meal down.

"Thank you," Luna called as it wheeled into the wall.

Luna sat down and savored her meal and coffee. It was delicious, and she didn't have to lift a finger. Alan walked in carrying a briefcase and handed Luna a tablet.

So, I have to go to work, and I'll be back at 4 with the lawyer to look at Beatrice's case. You can use the tablet to communicate with me and order anything you need. Can you make the house look presentable for him? I don't want him to see all of my stuff everywhere. "Ask Goddard if you need help with anything," Alan said.

"Okay, I will," Luna agreed. Are you going to eat your breakfast?

Alan checked his watch. I'm sorry, but I don't think I'll have time. Just place it in the refrigerator for me. I'll eat it later.

Luna was disappointed but forced a fake smile.

"Sure," she replied. Alan reached for the door but stopped.

Oh, before I forget. Make sure you stay here. "I'm not entirely sure if the Day Pass the welcome desk gave you is valid," Alan stated.

"Okay," Luna replied, waving as Alan rushed out the door.

Luna showered and bathed Oliver. She promptly dressed and started unloading all the boxes spread across the apartment. Oliver clapped and trilled in amusement as they worked. With the help of goddard, she unpacked all the boxes and watched one of the robots haul the empty cardboard boxes out of the apartment. Luna sat down on the couch and activated the tablet.

"How do I message Alan?" she asked the robot. The robot clicked on a chat bubble icon on the screen. Luna saw Alan's tube number and profile appear on the screen. *Maybe I can contact Harold to notify him about the lawyer*, Luna thought. She typed his tube number in the search bar, but no results popped up. Luna sighed in frustration.

Goddard, why can't I find this tube number?

The robot peered over at the screen.

Is he in the Star Sector?

"No," Luna responded.

Then, you have to use this app. He motioned to a water droplet icon on the home page. Luna saw her contact information pop up, as did Hoodi's. Luna's eyes lit up. No one had ever been able to message Hoodi directly. He always came to them when he wanted to do business. Luna studied Hoodi's tube number. *No wonder we couldn't find him. He has a Cloud Sector area code! That jerk doesn't even live in the Ocean Sector,* Luna fumed.

Goddard, can you write this number down on paper for me?

Certainly!

Luna read the tube number out loud, and the robot spit a paper from its mouth. Luna pulled out the paper and double-checked to ensure it matched the screen. She pulled out an address book and then returned to the couch. She added Hoodi's contact info to the book and added Harold's tube number to the search bar. Harold's contact information popped up, and the Land Sector sigil appeared in his profile picture. *I didn't know Harold was from the Land Sector,* Luna reflected. Perhaps she wasn't supposed to know that about him. She sent Harold a message notifying who she was and about the lawyer. A phone appeared on the screen.

Did I break it?

No, he's sending you a video call.

"Swipe right to answer," the robot instructed.

Harold's shriveled face appeared on the screen. Luna jumped in surprise.

"Luna, is that really you?" Harold exclaimed.

Yes. "Oliver and I are with Alan in the Star Sector," Luna responded and explained the events that had transpired.

"I'm so sorry," Harold apologized. But I'm glad you're safe.

Yes, and we might have found a good lawyer for Beatrice.

"That's wonderful, but I'm not sure if I can afford him," Harold mumbled.

Don't worry. We'll fight for a reasonable quote. "Can you send me a picture of the ticket and anything else the court has sent you?" Luna inquired.

I will, but that's the strange thing. I only have the ticket. The court hasn't set me, Jack. "It's weird. They won't let me see her either," Harold continued. Something isn't adding up. Luna's heart sank.

"Don't worry, the lawyer will sort it out," Luna reassured.

"Thank you, thank you," Harold cried. Call me if you need anything else. The Land sigil stuck in Luna's mind.

"Harold, why didn't you tell us you were from the Land Sector?" Luna asked.

Harold paused and looked whistful. It's a long story that happened a long time ago. Okay. "Maybe B and I will tell you one evening over drinks," he sighed.

This was not the repose Luna was hoping for.

"Have a good night, Luna, and stay safe," he said, ending the video call. An image of Beatrice's ticket appeared on the message board.

Goddard, are you able to print this?

The robot beeped and pulled out a printed copy of the ticket from the top of its head. Luna held the paper in admiration and placed it on the table.

You know you're amazing, right? The robot chimed and did a spin.

Alan and a man with a big nose entered the apartment. Goddard sprang forward and took their briefcases. He carried them to the next room. Luna stood up and forced a smile on her face. The man scanned the room and looked offended.

"Where's your furniture?" he remarked in a dismissive tone. It will arrive tomorrow. "I would like to introduce you to Luna and her son Oliver," Alan announced. They are good friends of the person I talked to you about at lunch.

Luna did a slight curt seat, and Oliver cooed in delight.

"Nice to meet you," Luna said.

The man's eyes flickered from Oliver to Alan, and he grimaced.

"Yes, of course," he sniffed, his black mustache twitching as he spoke. I'm Mr. Finnegan. I'm an attorney who has worked with Alan's family. What happened?

Luna handed over the photo of the ticket and explained what had happened to Beatrice. Mr. Finnegan studied the ticket and scoffed. I'm glad you contacted me. It looks like the people who put your friend in jail didn't do their job. "That's good news for us because that means she can be released due to a technicality," Mr. Finnegan remarked.

Luna beamed.

"That's wonderful news," she clapped. When do you think they will release her court date?

"Oh, there's no need," Mr. Finnegan mused. I know the judge. We're golf buddies, you see. The courts are all backed up, so just contacting him will be faster.

Mrs. Finnegan pulled out his phone and dialed. *Hey, Rich! It's Thomas. Would you be willing to drop a case for me really quick? The case number is 12679C3. Yes. Yes.* "Thank you," Mr. Finnegan said into the phone. He hung up the phone and grinned. She'll be released tomorrow. "Goddard, please print

Mrs. Beatrice Calwalds' discharge paperwork," Mr. Finnegan demanded.

Luna gaped at him. She and Harold had been struggling for months to get a trial set up for Beatrice, and Mr. Finnegan was able to get her released with just one phone call. Luna closed her mouth and tried not to burst into tears.

"Thank you," she breathed and wiped her eyes. How much do we owe you?

Owe me? It was no issue at all. No need to charge you. However, you can say something good about me to your aunt. "I would greatly appreciate it," Mr. Finnegan winked at Alan.

Alan pressed his lips together and said nothing.

"Oh, we will. I'm sure Aunt Debbie would be impressed with your quick thinking and skills," Luna lied.

"Exactly what I was thinking," Mr. Finnegan agreed. Mr. Finnegan pulled a paper from Goddards's head and handed it to Luna.

"Beatrice will be released at this time," he explained and pointed at the bottom of the paper.

Yes, I'll let her husband know. "Again, thank you," Luna gushed with a slight bow. Mr. Finnegan turned to leave and grabbed his belongings from Goddard.

Have a good night! "And stay out of trouble," he announced, squeezing Alan's shoulder.

Mr. Finegan departed, and Luna plopped on the couch.

"Did that really just happen?" she asked Alan.

"Yes, and I'm glad it all worked out," Alan responded and sat beside her.

Can you hold Oliver while I send this to Harold?

Alan picked up Oliver and cradled him. Luna activated the tablet and pulled up Harold's message board.

How do you take a picture with this thing?

"You know, you're such an old man when it comes to technology," Alan teased, pushing the camera icon at the bottom.

What! "We don't have all this fancy stuff in the Ocean Sector," Luna protested, sending Harold an image of the paperwork. I'm only teasing. Alan laughed and pulled her in. Luna put the tablet on the table and held his hands. She wanted to freeze time and stay in that moment forever. But like all good things, their time together was drawing to an end.

Chapter 20

CHOICES

Luna and Harold anxiously waited at the lobby room of the prison. Oliver squirmed and whimpered in her arms, sensing the unease that hung in the room. Luna kissed his forehead and hummed at him while Harold went to talk to the secretary in the front. A buzzer sounded, and an officer escorted out Beatrice. The officer checked the paperwork submitted by Harold and then uncuffed Beatrice. Harold and Beatrice hugged each other, and Harold became a blubbering mess. Tears and mucus streamed down his face. Beatrice patted his head and whispered kind words. Luna wanted to hug Beatrice but didn't want to interrupt the couple's tender moment. She was elated that her friend was finally free.

"Aww, who's this?" Beatrice gasped at Oliver.

Oliver waved his arms and cooed.

"Oh, he's so precious," Beatrice cried. Can I hold him?

Please!

Luna nodded and handed her son over.

"Let's talk outside," Luna suggested, looking pensively at the officers collaborating at the front. Luna and Harold followed Beatrice out of the station to the plastic transportation tube between buildings.

"This is Alan's and I's son," Luna whispered into Beatrice's ear. Beatrice's face dropped.

So how did your mother take it?

"Not well," Luna admitted and glanced down at the floor.

Does his family know?

Yes.

And you are not dead. "You are very lucky," Beatrice remarked.

Are you mad at me?

Beatrice stopped and turned towards her.

No. You're not dead yet, and I am free. "So, I will not let any news, no matter how shocking upset me," Beatrice smiled. Where is Safari? I thought she will be with you all. Luna and Harold exchanged concerned glances. Luna explained what happened with the House of Prosperity and Hoodi.

"That evil man is a blight on our lives," Beatrice snarled, and her face grew stern. I'm so sorry about your family and the fact I couldn't be there for you. "If you want, you can move in with us," Beatrice offered.

"Are you sure?" Luna squeaked. "Yes, we must stick together and fight," Beatrice fumed. I am not letting him get away with harming my family, and I'm tired of him terrorizing our community.

"Take it easy, B.

There is no need to get worked up," Harold soothed. Don't worry, once we find him. We are going to gut him like a fish. *The number!* Luna thought. *Oh no, I left it in my work bag with Alan.* She would have to show Beatrice later.

Beatrice swallowed hard to calm her nerves.

So, where are you and Oliver staying? So we can start moving your things.

"With Alan," Luna whispered. Beatrice hesitated.

How?

"It turns out that people bend the rules up there to get what they want," Luna hinted.

"He also helped you get out of jail," Harold added. He's different from those self-absorbed, rich idiots. I see why Luna likes him.

Beatrice flashed an annoyed look at her husband, and Luna smiled.

"So, are you going to stay with him?" Beatrice huffed.

I want to, but I know I can't.

"I don't belong in their world," Luna admitted. And I don't want him to leave his world for me. I just wish things were different. He's so loving and good with Oliver. I'm going to miss him.

"It will be alright in the end," Beatrice assured. Go to him and do what you need to do. Harold and I will take care of Oliver until you come back. Luna embraced Beatrice.

"Thank you," she whispered, for always being by my side.

***

Luna knocked on the apartment door, and Alan answered. She wrapped her arms around him and covered his face with kisses.

"Well, that was a pleasant surprise," he murmured in admiration. They clung to each other briefly.

Where's Oliver?

"I left him with Beatrice," Luna informed him, rubbing his shoulders. His face fell.

"Oh, I take it everything went well," he said.

"Yes, thanks to you," Luna replied, kissing his forehead.

"So, you're leaving," Alan croaked, his eyes watered.

I'm sorry, Alan. But I can't stay here forever.

"I wish you could," he breathed. His face filled with pain.

I love you, and you're a great father to Oliver. "Us living in different places won't change that," Luna soothed and rubbed his arms. Alan looked at the floor, lost for words.

"Wait here, I want to give you something before you go," he said and disappeared into the other room. Luna's heart ached and fanned her face to stop herself from crying. She tossed her work bag over her back and waited. Alan placed a silver necklace with a ring on it into her palm. Luna studied the ring. A pearl gleamed in the center. Luna recognized it from the Deep-Sea Aquarium.

"What is this for?" Luna asked, blinking away tears. Alan unclipped the necklace and positioned it around her neck.

"It's a promise," he explained. We can't legally get married right now, but I love you. And I want you to be my wife.

"It's a little late for you to make me an honest woman," Luna said, tears streaming down her face.

Alan pressed his forehead against her and held the ring up.

When you feel alone, I want you to look at this and think of me. Luna knew their love was real and invincible to what society had to say about them.

"Goodbye, husband," she whispered. They kiss for a final time, their tears mingling as their cheeks touch. Luna stowed the ring on the inside of her shirt and returned to her home.